AUTHORITY
MARKETING FOR DENTISTS

Your Blueprint to Build Thought Leadership That Grows
Your Practice, Attracts Patients, and Makes Competition Irrelevant

---

ADAM WITTY | RUSTY SHELTON

Published by ForbesBooks, Charleston, South Carolina.
Member of Advantage Media Group.

ForbesBooks is a registered trademark, and the ForbesBooks colophon is a trademark of Forbes Media, LLC.

Printed in the United States of America.

10 9 8 7 6 5 4 3 2 1

ISBN: 978-1-950863-65-5
LCCN: 2020917613

Cover and layout design by George Stevens.

This publication is designed to provide accurate and authoritative information in regard to the subject matter covered. It is sold with the understanding that the publisher is not engaged in rendering legal, accounting, or other professional services. If legal advice or other expert assistance is required, the services of a competent professional person should be sought.

 Advantage Media Group is proud to be a part of the Tree Neutral® program. Tree Neutral offsets the number of trees consumed in the production and printing of this book by taking proactive steps such as planting trees in direct proportion to the number of trees used to print books. To learn more about Tree Neutral, please visit www.treeneutral.com.

Since 1917, the Forbes mission has remained constant. Global Champions of Entrepreneurial Capitalism. ForbesBooks exists to further that aim by bringing the Stories, Passion, and Knowledge of top thought leaders to the forefront. ForbesBooks brings you The Best in Business. To be considered for publication, please visit www.forbesbooks.com.

AUTHORITY

MARKETING FOR DENTISTS

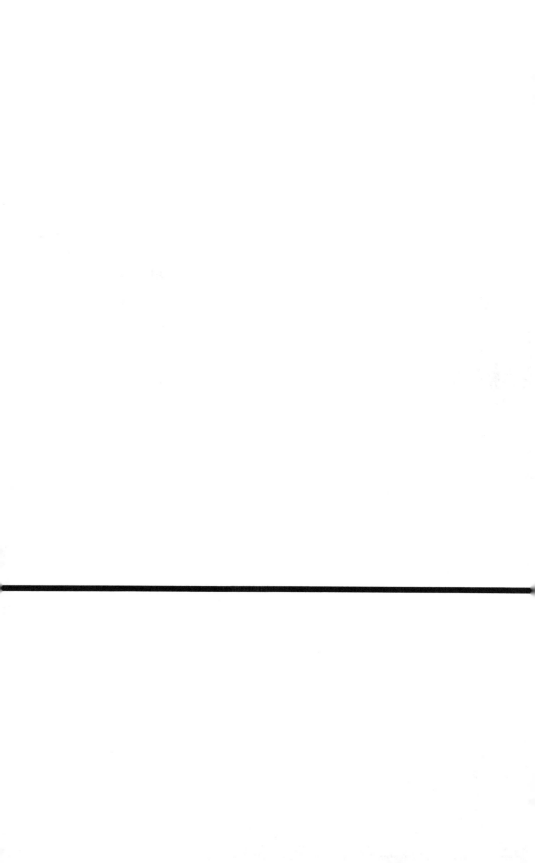

This book is dedicated to dentists, practice managers,
and oral health professionals who have Stories, Passion,
and Knowledge to share with the world.

Visit us online to access these free resources:

Find Out Your Patient Relationship Score.

We've created a simple 9 Question Assessment that will reveal your Patient Relationship Score in under 3 minutes, and share with you exactly how you can quickly improve your score.

→ Take the Patient Relationship Assessment by visiting at mlivesoftware.com/assessment.

SUBSCRIBE to Dental Marketing Live.

You've learned about the Seven Pillars of Authority Marketing, now stay on top of the latest marketing trends and strategies with the mLive Dental Marketing weekly newsletter. Read articles and latest dental industry trends to stay on top of your marketing efforts.

→ Subscribe at mlivesoftware.com/newsletter.

Book a Complimentary Demo of our mLive Software.

Learn how you can easily attract and win over more, new, and better patients with our bold, persuasive automated marketing campaigns. mLive Dental Marketing Automation software does all this and more so you can put your marketing on autopilot.

→ Schedule today at mlivesoftware.com/demo.

CONTENTS

Foreword ix
  by Steve Forbes

Preface xiii

PART I 1
THE BIG IDEA

  What is Authority Marketing? 3

  The Three Eras of Authority Marketing . .15

  The Case for Authority Marketing 25

Part II 27
**BUILDING YOUR BLUEPRINT:
THE FOUNDATION, PILLARS, AND
OUTCOMES OF AUTHORITY MARKETING**

  The Foundation of Authority 29

    You Can't Spell Authority Without AUTHOR 29

  The Pillars of Authority 43

    Branding and Omnipresence .45

    Content Marketing 57

PR and Media 81

Speaking. 87

The Outcomes of Authority 93

Lead Generation 93

Patient Conversion. 97

Retention / Referrals 103

Part III 117

IMPLEMENTING YOUR AUTHORITY MARKETING BLUEPRINT

Beginning with the
End in Mind 119

Happiness and Authority Marketing 131

Afterword: The Power of Authority 139
by Dan Kennedy, *Founder of Magnetic Marketing*

About the Authors 149

FOREWORD

by Steve Forbes

"All I need is a sheet of paper and something to write with, and then I can turn the world upside down." —*Friedrich Nietzsche*

There is no secret formula for great leadership. However, there are certain timeless attributes: the ability to inspire trust, to impart a vision and sense of direction, to make hard decisions and see that they are carried out, and to develop the art of delegating instead of trying to do everything yourself. This, in turn, means picking capable people for carrying out particular tasks and constantly evaluating their performances. Understanding their strengths and limitations is crucial. Great leaders are crisis managers, which may mean having to deal with problems for which there is no "playbook," that is, no obvious solutions and answers. Inevitably, mistakes will be made, though great leaders learn how to rebound and move ahead.

Very importantly, outstanding leaders strive to do big things that can turn conventional wisdom on its head. This, of course, is going for the high risk. A wannabe great leader, overcome by timidity and the desire to play it safe, is bound for forgettable mediocrity.

While all of these factors have been known since the dawn of recorded history, there are only a relative handful of individuals in each generation who are willing to step up and take the reins.

You want to be one of them. As you pursue your bold ambitions, you understand that complacency is death. As one scholar of leadership has put it, to not make a resounding impact in your field is akin to dying on your knees instead of on your feet. In today's environment, leadership is amplified by authority and there is no room in this world for uncertain authority; it's a contradiction. Now, here comes a crucial point: authority cannot be achieved quietly. If you want to be seen as a thought leader in your field—a person of outstanding authority whose observations are accorded instant respect, whose pieces of advice are almost treated as prescriptions, and who makes such a positive impact that they leave a lasting legacy—then you need to make it clearly known.

And one of the most powerful ways to achieve this rare stature is through book authorship. Over the years I have written several books and coauthored or edited others. Each in its own way has underscored those vital elements of leadership mentioned above. They have sharply challenged conventional wisdom. They established a foundation of trust by conveying solid fact over myth. Furthermore, people are inspired to take action when they better understand the American political and economic climate.

But in today's media landscape, the journey to becoming an authority isn't complete with a book, just like the journey for Forbes to become a modern global business and media brand wasn't limited to a print magazine. I encourage you to be bold and embrace the same innovative "media" mindset that we have fostered at Forbes for more than a century. Just like we went beyond the magazine to reach our audience in new ways, Adam and Rusty will teach you how you can integrate rented, earned, and owned media to build an audience for your message in a bold and transformational way.

The value of firmly establishing your authority in your field cannot be overstated. Sharing your unique perspective within your field is one of the most direct and powerful ways to make this happen. It is your vehicle to drive real and lasting change.

Bottom line: people have to know you're there. And this book will show you the way to do it.

PREFACE

In the spring of 2015, Advantage|Business Journals Books|ForbesBooks founder and CEO, Adam Witty, took a step back to try to identify the macro trends that would shape the marketing world in the years to come. At the time, the company he founded more than a decade before in 2005, Advantage Media Group, had helped hundreds of entrepreneurs, CEOs, and professionals create and publish a book to help grow their business. Although the company was incredibly successful and won numerous awards for rapid growth, quality, and culture, he believed publishing books was only scratching the surface of the ways he could impact his authors, because the company didn't provide a marketing framework that could be reliably executed.

As you know, because you chose to pick up this book, there is no shortage of options when it comes to marketing. Adam felt like a shift was taking place that was putting more power in the hands of you—the expert. Rather than having to do what everyone else is doing by focusing on the expensive, time-intensive, and unreliable process needed to build a corporate brand, you could control your own marketing destiny.

How did he know a shift was taking place?

He saw it happening in his own life.

When Adam founded Advantage, he did what most entrepreneurs and business leaders do—he focused on building the company's corporate brand. He was successful by most metrics, growing the company at a significant rate, but he was plagued with significant competition from other publishers. The company didn't truly hit "lift-off" until he started focusing on something none of his competitors were focused on—a personal brand. He knew he didn't have the marketing budget or brand name in place that large publishers had and decided the quickest and most effective route to success was to focus on building his own personal brand as a way to amplify the Advantage brand. As a result, he was named to the *Inc.* magazine 30 Under 30 list in 2011, wrote numerous books, began speaking at EO, YPO, and Vistage events and made it a point to personally be involved in author events around the country.

The impact on the business of this shift to Authority-building has been significant. Revenues have grown tenfold and the visibility Adam built opened the door for a partnership deal between Advantage Media Group and Forbes to launch the company's first-ever book publishing imprint, ForbesBooks.

Adam recognized that he was playing a game none of his competitors knew was being played by building his personal Authority and that Authority Marketing® was the most important macro trend entrepreneurs, CEOs, and professionals needed to pay attention to.

He decided the best way to help authors was through an acquisition and he went on a nationwide hunt for the top thought leadership agency in the country. That search quickly led him to Rusty Shelton, who was running Shelton Interactive, an award-winning agency that represented more than thirty-five *New York Times* and

Wall Street Journal bestsellers, including clients like Keller Williams Realty cofounder Gary Keller, Chicken Soup for the Soul, and numerous other global brands. A published author himself, Rusty had been building his own Authority, first speaking at Harvard on the changing world of PR and marketing at the age of twenty-three and a veteran speaker of many other elite conferences, including SXSW.

Adam and Rusty quickly hit it off and joined forces to build the Authority Marketing System that has helped numerous experts build their Authority, expand their impact, and, ultimately, make their competition irrelevant.

The book you're about to read will teach you how to utilize Authority Marketing to take your dental practice to the next level.

—Adam Witty and Rusty Shelton

 LEAD GENERATION

$ PATIENT CONVERSION

BRANDING + OMNIPRESENCE

CONTENT MARKETING

PR + MEDIA

FOUNDATION OF AUTHORITY
JOURNEY TITLE

BOOK AUTHORSHIP

ETENTION / REFERRALS

SPEAKING

PART I

THE BIG IDEA

WHAT IS AUTHORITY MARKETING?

When he set out to make an impact in the field of dental sleep medicine, Dr. Daniel Klauer probably didn't imagine that one day he'd be hosting "immersion days" at his practice for colleagues, or lending his materials on "proven processes" to inspire practices all over the country to develop their own strategic plans for success. All those years ago when he was first starting out, his current reality probably felt like it was light years—and a whole lot of hard work—away.

So how did Dr. Klauer become a sought-after leader in his field—and a consultant who helps other dentists build thoughtful plans for profitable practices? He adopted the principles of Authority Marketing, and he did it at a pivotal moment in his career. His transition from run-of-the-mill practitioner with big dreams into a person with influence in his subject and his field happened because he made key moves early in his career that set him apart from competitors.

Dr. Klauer is a TMJ and sleep therapy specialist from Indiana who has consistently used the pillars of Authority Marketing to his greatest advantage. Before Dr. Klauer encountered Authority Marketing, he and his team had just moved into a new building. They had the space and the platform to grow as a team and as a practice— even branching out to share their message with other providers in the area. As Dr. Klauer began to see more and more patients for sleep and pain management, he found he was often repeating the same message over and over again. He enjoyed introducing patients to the world of dental sleep medicine, but he needed to streamline his approach and help patients at the same time.

It was on a trip to Charleston that Dr. Klauer first learned about Authority Marketing. On a tour of the Advantage|Business Journals Books|ForbesBooks headquarters, Dr. Klauer met with Adam and other Advantage|Business Journals Books|ForbesBooks associates, where he learned how to utilize his narrative and his journey to the benefit of his practice. He learned how to get his story and his mission in the hands of patients before they walked through the door—and he did this by writing a book.

But writing a book is about more than just producing and publishing a manuscript; it's about knowing how to utilize what you write. The payoff for Dr. Klauer has been absolutely essential to his practice's growth. His book has been a resource for new and prospective patients, a tool for other doctors and dentists, and it has allowed him to share his success strategies with others. "It's been way more than just a book," Dr. Klauer notes. "It's been a mindset shift and it's made a huge impact on my personal goals and ambitions."

When Dr. Klauer's patients schedule an appointment with him, they're immediately sent the chapter of his book, *Achieve Your Victory: Solutions for TMD and Sleep Apnea,* that is most relevant to them.

When time permits, they're sent a physical copy in the mail. That way, they can have a tangible and enlightening piece of literature to familiarize themselves with before coming in. They can read patient stories, become familiar with Dr. Klauer's approaches and values, and begin to see the possibilities for their own treatment. Along with that immediate value for patients comes value for Dr. Klauer's practice—his patients see him as an Authority before they even walk through the door.

The Authority that Dr. Klauer has built extends beyond being a published author—it shows up in his online presence, media appearances, high-profile speaking engagements, and in his reputation among other practitioners. In a field as competitive as his, he has managed to triple the credibility he already held through his credentials and education alone. His social and digital footprints add the authority and credibility that he needs to make a lasting impact on existing and potential patients. Most importantly, by following the tenets that we will lay out in *Authority Marketing for Dentists*, Dr. Klauer has served thousands—in his community and far beyond.

So, what do we mean by *Authority?*

Authority occurs when someone takes the right steps to combine standout, *trustworthy* expertise in his or her field with the kind of high visibility you might often associate with a *celebrity*. When that happens, the expert's name becomes synonymous with the field he or she works in—which of course provides an incalculable advantage over competitors.

But even though the advantage is incalculable, the blueprint formula for building it is fairly straightforward:

AUTHORITY = EXPERTISE x CELEBRITY

If the mere mention of the word "celebrity" makes you want to put this book down, we understand—but hang tight while we unpack what we mean by celebrity. We don't mean "household name" celebrity or a me-first ego-driven celebrity. Instead, we're talking about the kind of high-impact visibility and third-party credibility that causes you—the expert—to be viewed as a mission-driven thought leader in your specific niche or field.

In this book you'll read about numerous authorities—formerly unknown experts who've gone on to make millions of dollars and impact countless lives by becoming *well-known* experts in their field. Ones like Dr. Klauer.

The good news is that it's never been easier to build Authority and use it to accelerate the speed of trust. In today's media environment—which is driven in large part by discoverability and brand building pre-engagement—when you combine great knowledge and expertise with celebrity-style visibility, you are perceived as far more than just another expert that someone can shop on price against competitors. Instead, you are seen as the go-to thought leader in your field! Someone with whom any prospect would feel fortunate to even get an appointment.

Authority doesn't just happen to you—it's the result of a specific process called Authority Marketing, which builds your visibility and credibility in your field and uses that thought leadership as a way to drive business and make a bigger impact. Doing this creates a wonderfully unfair advantage over your competitors, which reminds us of Dr. Klauer's cultivation of both his personal and professional brands. Through branding, he further cements—and makes available to the public eye—the Authority that comes with being one of the best in his field.

AUTHORITY MARKETING BUILDS YOUR VISIBILITY AND CREDIBILITY IN YOUR FIELD AND USES THAT THOUGHT LEADERSHIP AS A WAY TO DRIVE BUSINESS AND MAKE A BIGGER IMPACT.

The recognition that Dr. Klauer has accumulated—through his book, through his engagement efforts, and with his rigorous follow-through—have led to innumerable opportunities for growth. He has been a keynote speaker at a conference with over a thousand orthodontists for two years in a row, and regularly helps other dentists find their passion and develop their mission.

As for marketing efforts—Dr. Klauer has been hard at work in that area, too. He "owns his real estate" when it comes to media—a concept we'll talk in depth about later in the book—and he knows how to use social media to complement his personal and professional personas. All of these factors combine to make Dr. Klauer a trusted and respected leader in his field—someone who journalists and news outlets seek out when they need an Authority in dentistry to share advice with the public.

Dr. Klauer is one of many examples of the power of Authority Marketing and how it can be used to transform careers and change lives. He went from a leader in an up-and-coming field within dentistry, competing against thousands of other dentists, to a noted Authority whose advice and "blueprint" for success is sought after and utilized by many.

A PERSONAL BRAND ACCELERATES TRUST

Everyone understands the value of having a visible, respected corporate brand, but few understand the power of a *personal* brand.

Most entrepreneurs, dentists, and doctors launch a business and focus on building visibility or equity for the corporate logo and name, whether it be through high-end graphic design, expensive advertising campaigns, a dominant social-media presence, or even PR. When you focus on your corporate brand, you are not only playing a game everyone else is playing, you're often playing against some of the most established and branded practices in the nation. When you go head-to-head with large, established brands you often fight a losing battle, as you're chasing a brand that has a several decades' head start in terms of awareness, and often a marketing budget that dwarfs yours. This is a fool's errand, as you just don't have the resources or name recognition to compete with the biggest in the industry.

But Authority Marketing levels the playing field by focusing on an individual Authority brand: meaning that you essentially become your own brand. Against the backdrop of a marketplace that is increasingly skeptical of large corporate brands, Authority Marketing accelerates the speed of trust like nothing else.

AUTHORITY MARKETING LEVELS THE PLAYING FIELD BY FOCUSING ON AN INDIVIDUAL AUTHORITY BRAND: MEANING THAT YOU ESSENTIALLY BECOME YOUR OWN BRAND.

Imagine a potential patient has decided to choose a new provider. She's asking friends and doctors for recommendations, she's using search engines, and she's likely using social media. She's narrowed her search down to four dentists in her area who are specialists in the area she needs work in. Assuming each is trustworthy and has an accredited practice, what makes one stand out against another, especially if each is associated with established practices? Not much, right?

What if one of the four, Dr. Carrie Wheeler, is an active speaker in town and has been frequently quoted by local media? When the patient—Rachel—visits her website and Facebook page during her decision-making process, she notices that Dr. Wheeler is a media personality, keynote speaker, and even a published author. This initial impression of third-party Authority accelerates the speed of trust and completely changes the dynamics of Rachel's search: Dr. Wheeler has already established her Authority before Rachel even makes an appointment. Instead of feeling like her choice is a shot in the dark, Rachel feels fortunate to have gotten an appointment with such an Authority. This dentist now has a significant edge, as she's marketing her Authority and commanding respect instead of only trying to attract business.

The single most valuable benefit to becoming an Authority is accelerating the speed of trust. When you do so, you're not seen as someone who has something to sell, but instead as a thought leader that has something to teach. The key is to use Authority to establish trust before you ever sit down with someone. When you do this, you don't have to establish your credibility or make the case as to why you're the best resource; you can go right to problem solving and, as such, people are more willing to take your recommendations. In other words, Authority reduces the sales cycle. Oftentimes, that means potential patients shop around less, if at all. They feel lucky to be talking to you and are going with you because of who you are rather than what you offer—because you have demonstrated that you are a *trustworthy* practitioner.

This works in any field. Imagine a local entrepreneur is looking for a new financial advisor. She's interviewing four candidates, each of whom has the expertise and experience necessary to earn the business and provide sound financial advice. As she's reviewing credentials, she notices that one of the four has keynoted at a well-known conference several years in a row, has appeared on national television, and has written a book. The third-party credibility established differentiates this candidate from their competitors, causing the entrepreneur to view them as an established Authority before they even meet. The entrepreneur trusts that person's capabilities almost immediately, and chances are, she's going to feel lucky to have

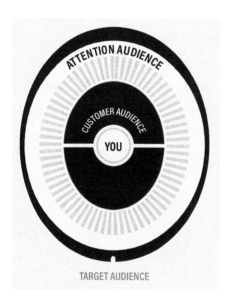

TARGET AUDIENCE

them as her financial advisor. That's the kind of competitive edge that being an Authority provides.

YOUR BLUEPRINT

In this book, we will provide a blueprint to build your **Authority Coliseum**. Your coliseum will stand the test of time and benefit you for the rest of your professional career.

Authority is built on a strong foundation of **Book Authorship**. That foundation supports authority pillars of **Branding + Omnipresence**, **Content Marketing, PR + Media,** and **Speaking**. The outcomes of having authority are numerous. Authority improves **Lead Generation, Sales Conversion,** and **Retention/Referrals**. These positive outcomes, desired by all practitioners, entrepreneurs, and business professionals, are made possible by your authority foundation and pillars. In total, this is the Authority Coliseum you will be able to build for yourself by following our blueprint.

EFFECTIVE AUTHORITY MARKETING INVOLVES A STRATEGIC PROCESS OF SYSTEMATICALLY POSITIONING A PERSON AS THE LEADER AND EXPERT IN THE DENTAL INDUSTRY, COMMUNITY, AND MARKETPLACE TO COMMAND AN OUTSIZED INFLUENCE AND EDGE ON COMPETITORS.

Remember, Authority doesn't just happen—effective Authority Marketing involves a strategic process of systematically positioning a person as the leader and expert in the dental industry, community, and marketplace to command an outsized influence and edge on competitors. A strategic process means creating a deliberate plan, which is executed over a specific period of time. This eliminates ad hoc questions like, "What do we need to do today?" or "How should we tackle this next month?" Authority Marketing requires a clearly defined blueprint that is implemented methodically over time. It is only through deliberate intention and disciplined action that real Authority can be gained.

Systematic positioning—the implementation of your blueprint in such a way as to provide the most effective return on investment possible—goes hand-in-hand with strategic process. If you're practicing law in Cleveland, Ohio, you're not going to get much mileage from local TV in San Antonio or Atlanta. You wouldn't waste your time pitching news stories to the *Los Angeles Times*. Rather, you would focus your efforts in your practice's prime radius, then work to ensure you become known in every aspect of that area's most visible media. As we will talk about later in this book, the credibility that comes with national media is very important, but for many businesses, local media provides the most direct impact on Authority. This is about more than brand recognition—you don't just want people to know the name of your practice; you want them to see or hear the name and say, "Hey, I have been hearing a lot about that person."

The reality of any practice or business comes down to competition. You're competing in a marketplace, an industry, and a community. Coming out on top is all about the sway you have over and above other practices to help you influence people toward your services. Your blueprint needs to be designed to achieve just that. (Much more about this starting in Part II.)

Entrepreneur Ben Compaine once said, "The marketplace is not a podium in a quiet lecture hall where everyone gets a turn to speak. It's more like a crowded bazaar in Casablanca. You must distract people from their main occupation—living—and show them that they can't live a minute longer without one of your beautiful rugs."

When you and your practice are *the* Authority in your region, you have a powerful microphone and platform in that crowded bazaar, and that wonderfully unfair advantage makes all the difference, because it allows you to stand out above your competition.

Done properly, Authority Marketing isn't about ego or attention—it's about affinity, which equals trust, and it turns you and your business into a magnet for potential patients, rather than you needing to go out and sell yourself to them one at a time. This book is about showing you how to do just that.

THE THREE ERAS OF
AUTHORITY MARKETING

Although it may sound like a new concept, the story of Authority Marketing is as old as civilization. In ancient Rome, Authority derived from titles. Men of the Senate or the Plebeian Council were seen as *the* Authorities on matters of the state and public life. To become such an Authority, one needed to be a born member of the Patrician class or be a skilled orator who could effectively speak to the masses and be elected to the Plebeian Council. In either case, it was the official status bestowed by the Roman state that conferred Authority.

Such is the way it went for much of history—if you wanted Authority, it had to be officially bestowed upon you by the state, monarchy, or institution of social significance. The English government would extend it to individuals outside of government with official titles and honors, such as knighthood. These individuals enjoyed public trust, notoriety, and preference as a result. However, there was a flipside for all of those who weren't fortunate enough to have such Authority bestowed upon them and, for most, it meant a life of limited opportunity.

Centuries later, with the advent of mass media, the dynamic began to change. Looking back, we can now categorize the evolution of true Authority Marketing into three distinct eras. In the first era, pre-1875, Authority had to be officially bestowed by a formal Authority, whether that be a government body, monarch, or social institution. In the second era, roughly 1875–2000, the media gained the power and ability to crown individuals with Authority. Now, in the digital age, we have seen the democratization of media, and with that the dawn of a third era of Authority Marketing. Today, you can establish yourself as an Authority by serving your audience. This is the revolutionary power of the new media landscape.

TODAY, YOU CAN ESTABLISH YOURSELF AS AN AUTHORITY BY SERVING YOUR AUDIENCE. THIS IS THE REVOLUTIONARY POWER OF THE NEW MEDIA LANDSCAPE.

Before we dig in on the opportunities presented in our current era, let's look back at the first two to provide a foundation for our current opportunity.

ERA ONE – INSTITUTIONAL AUTHORITY (PRE-1875)

Marcus Tullius Cicero was one of Rome's most famous figures. He was a member of the Patrician class, a politician, and a lawyer, who served as consul in 63 BC. He was able to rise to Rome's highest position for two reasons: his noble birth and his tremendous oratory skills. Cicero was born with Authority and was able to command more of it through his ability to communicate with the masses.

Cicero's oratory was so influential, he had a significant impact on the Latin language, affecting its style and prose. Imagine having so much Authority that the way you spoke changed the very language for everyone.

There were several other prominent Roman figures who used the Authority of their state titles to spread their influence—most notably Gaius Julius Caesar. It was through his Authority and influence that Caesar transformed Rome from a republic to an empire, and in so doing made himself a figure of worldwide significance. To this day, variations of his name are used as titles to confer Authority and power, such as *czar*.

Caesar's name carried such clout that his nephew and successor, Octavian, took it as his own, adopting the name Augustus Caesar. Augustus went so far as to have two months of the year renamed in honor of his late uncle and himself; July for Julius, August for Augustus. *Now that's Authority Marketing!*

Social institutions, such as the Catholic Church, were also sources of Authority during the first era of Authority Marketing. The advent of the printing press, in 1440, furthered the Church's influence by facilitating the wide distribution of the most influential book of all time: the Bible. The spreading of Christianity, thanks in no small part to the Bible, led the Church to such high levels of power, it rivaled states and monarchies. This created conflict with those seeking to compete with or contest the Church's Authority.

While the Pope has always been a social and spiritual Authority, King Henry VIII famously challenged it in 1534, after Pope Clement VII refused to annul his marriage to Catherine of Aragon. With a little help from Martin Luther and later John Calvin, the resulting Protestant Reformation significantly shifted the balance of social and spiritual Authority and resulted in many subsequent conflicts and wars.

These examples demonstrate not only how Authority was conferred throughout most of history but also how incredibly valuable it was. It was synonymous with power and influence, and in this era many died in disputes over it. Even the United States experienced such conflict, as the nation was forged by men of burgeoning Authority contesting that of others.

George Washington was the father of the United States and one of its most revered historical figures. When the Continental Congress needed a man to lead the colonial army against the crown, they called on General Washington. He was their natural choice as a man of high social stature, a decorated veteran, and a Freemason (another social institution capable of bestowing Authority by association). The American Revolution was a challenge to the Authority and power that Great Britain held over the American colonies. When Washington was victorious, he was the logical pick to be the first US president—precisely because his Authority and success on the battlefield had established him as a man of trust with the people.

Like the Catholic Church, the American patriots also used the printing press to gain Authority and influence. It was the wide distribution of Thomas Paine's *Common Sense* which converted many colonists to the cause of American independence. Such was the power of the press, which would be radically amplified with the advent of offset printing in 1875. It was offset printing that made mass distribution easy and affordable, leading to the rise of mainstream media. The influence and power of mainstream media would effectively end the monopoly social institutions and government had held on the ability to bestow Authority for all of civilization.

ERA TWO – MEDIA-DRIVEN AUTHORITY (1875–2000)

When we think about the second era of Authority Marketing, a few names stand out as the most notable. Their names were their brands and their successes were amplified by their ability to build those brands through mass-media coverage. This was an era that saw the rise of promoters and entertainers, like Harry Houdini and P.T. Barnum, to become household names.

Houdini used daring feats and spectacles to create fascination around his magic act. He would perform death-defying acts and contacted the press ahead of time to ensure crowds. His stunts were so dangerous that if he made mistakes, he could have been killed in front of everyone. But that suspense drew in eager spectators. He had confidence in his abilities and knew how to grab people's attention—it was all a thought-out, strategic, and systematic way for him to build Authority.

P.T. Barnum also understood how to create a spectacle. Barnum dubbed his traveling circus "The Greatest Show on Earth." Maybe you've heard of it? Some called it audacious at the time, but Barnum was a larger-than-life marketer who understood the value that came with such a brand. His show included exotic animals, lion tamers, and death-defying stunts. He also played on the morbid curiosities of his audiences with his freak show. In every city and town the show went to, people were clamoring to see it.

These experts were able to generate such buzz around their names that the press began to follow their every move, cementing their positions as the preeminent entertainers of their time. Newspapers were always reporting on Houdini's latest death-defying stunt and on Barnum's newest addition to his show. That's how Authority was minted in the second era of Authority Marketing—experts had to capture the attention of the press and use it to their advantage.

One leader who understood this better than any other politician of the era was Theodore Roosevelt. Generally ranked among the five greatest presidents in US history, Roosevelt was a statesman, author, explorer, and soldier who became a driving force in the progressive era of US politics. He began his rise to prominence by authoring a book, *The Naval War of 1812*, which established his reputation as a writer and a noted historian. From there, he masterfully built and marketed his Authority.

Roosevelt created a brand for himself centered on his exuberant personality, crafting a cowboy persona of rugged masculinity. This persona was a marketing tool he used to capture the attention of the press and, thus, the public. Roosevelt understood how to garner press coverage and use it to his advantage, coining the term "the bully pulpit" and using favorable press coverage to win people to his cause as president and spearhead his ambitious domestic and international agenda while in office.

There were also prominent business figures who achieved such massive financial success that, with the help of media amplification, they established an Authority which actually rivaled or exceeded that of politicians of the time. Men like J.P. Morgan, Andrew Carnegie, and John D. Rockefeller were known as titans of business—their very names synonymous with the industries they dominated. Rockefeller's name even became a household term for wealth.

ERA THREE – MARKET-DRIVEN AUTHORITY (2000–PRESENT)

With the advent of personal computing and the digitalization of media, Authority Marketing began another shift toward the end of the twentieth century. This new era would mark the dilution of the distribution monopoly traditional media held for more than a century, and, in so doing, bring about tremendous democratization of Authority Marketing. (Which is good news for you and everyone else reading this book.)

In the third era of Authority Marketing you don't have to wait for the media's blessing to begin building your Authority, although as we'll discuss in this book at length, it certainly accelerates the process. Instead, technology has empowered you to go around "traditional" media and build a direct connection with your audience that you personally own.

What's remarkable about this third era is that your audience is as interested in pushing "traditional" media out of the way to get to good Micromedia content as you are in providing it to them. This shift from the public is due to two factors:

1. They are increasingly skeptical of content delivered to them by large media outlets and that lack of trust has them looking elsewhere.

2. When they give their attention to large, generic media outlets they get only a fractional return on that investment. For example, if you like college sports...and more specifically college football...and even more specifically the Michigan Wolverines you could either listen to national sports radio where you'll have to deal with lots of other sports content or you can listen to a Michigan football podcast that gives

you a 1-to-1 return on your investment of time. The same is true across our interests, from finance to health, and the third era of Authority Marketing positions you to provide that content.

A book on Authority Marketing wouldn't be complete without a look at perhaps the most high-profile example of the new era of Authority Marketing: President Donald Trump. We almost didn't include this example because it has nothing to do with policies or politics. Whether you love him or hate him, his mastery of Authority Marketing is without rival. Trump is not new to this game; in fact, he began his career in the second era of Authority marketing and deftly adjusted to the landscape of the third era.

Throughout the 1980s and '90s, Trump crafted his personal brand and established his Authority as a business leader and real estate mogul. His book, *The Art of the Deal*, cemented him as an Authority on business in the minds of many Americans. The name Trump became synonymous with wealth and success. To ensure that, Trump put his name on as many buildings as he could. He wasn't concerned with drab real estate like office buildings—he put his name on casinos, golf courses, and luxury hotels, such as the Trump Taj Mahal, Trump National, and Trump Palace.

Trump understood the key to success in the second era of Authority Marketing was capturing widespread media attention, and he did that well. But he was also ahead of his time when it came to marketing his own personal Authority, something that supported his previously unthinkable success in the third era. His entire career has been calculated to craft a public image and build success off that image. *The Art of the Deal* is pretty much the campaign manifesto he would use thirty years later to win the presidency.

His larger-than-life Authority, plus the name recognition and corresponding audience he was able to bring with him, made Trump an attractive pick for NBC when they wanted to launch their reality TV show, *The Apprentice*. This showcases the shift from the second to the third era of Authority Marketing. In this instance, traditional media was using Trump's brand to bolster the Authority of this new show (that didn't yet have a brand). In turn, Trump used the television media platform to transform himself from a successful business executive to a full-fledged celebrity.

Trump then exponentially expanded his growing Authority through his use of social media. He used his Twitter account as a direct conduit to the public, going around the media to build affinity and generate attention from his audience to the point that even though many traditional media outlets on both the left and the right tried to stop him in his quest for the presidency—they failed. Counterintuitively, the more the media pushed against him, the stronger Trump's Authority became.

Ironically, although it was a combination of earned media (media coverage) and rented media (social media) that took him into the stratosphere of Authority, his journey toward a larger-than-life persona actually began with a book. He leveraged differential branding and savvy use of both traditional and social media to establish himself as an Authority—first through books, then speaking and real estate, and then through TV and social media—and he leveraged that Authority all the way to the White House. Whether you love him or hate him isn't the point; the reality is that there is a lot to learn from him when it comes to growing your business and making an impact with your message. In Washington, DC, a place still filled largely with older men from another era, Trump's understanding of the new media landscape is unique. That is why so many don't understand him or his popularity.

While it was possible in the second era of Authority Marketing for an individual to gain publicity on his or her own, the media held the power to establish or squash that Authority. Now, media has been democratized; as Trump has proven, a Twitter account used the right way can be more powerful than the world's biggest media outlets or established institutions.

In this new landscape, the power is truly in your hands—and it's up to you to establish yourself as an Authority to make sure your message is heard.

THE CASE FOR AUTHORITY MARKETING

lthough we—the authors and our firm, Advantage|Business Journals Books|ForbesBooks— believe there has never been a better time to establish Authority, the frank reality is that if you want to build a successful business and get your message out, there's never been a more important time to do it. In this age of online discoverability, the longer you wait to get intentional about building your brand, the further you fall behind competitors who are working hard to gain an outsized, not-so-wonderful advantage against *you*.

The reason Authority Marketing is so critically important to your business today is that in our current digital environment, the first impression most people will have of you and your brand won't happen in person or even over the phone—it will happen online, via page one of Google, your website, and social-media channels.

What's crazy is that this is even true when you are meeting someone in person! Think about it; if you are meeting a local business owner for coffee, what do you do in your car before you walk in the door? If you're like us and many people we know, you're scrolling through Google results for that person's name, reviewing his or her LinkedIn profile, and even clicking on that one-star review that caught your eye—all the while forming a first impression of that person in the five-minute review before you even walk through the door—an impression that will be hard for that person to change in the sixty minutes you spend together over coffee.

In this third era of Authority Marketing, your brand is, in large part, what Google says it is. When people meet you or speak with you on the phone, you should expect that their first impression has most likely already been established. Which makes owning it and ensuring it is congruent with the value you bring to the table your most important marketing mission.

As such, Authority is no longer just your ability to own the room, your degrees on the wall, or your years of hard-earned experience. In today's media landscape, Authority must be intentionally amplified online to ensure that the brand image you project presents you as the Authority you are.

If what we're saying sounds familiar, you have picked up the right book. Authority Marketing is the most underutilized strategy in today's media landscape. In the rest of this book, we will show you exactly how to implement it in your business life by taking the same kind of intentional, strategic approach that has been successful in delivering your product or service—and applying the same systematic, high-caliber mindset toward marketing your Authority.

How do you do that? Let's get started building your Authority Marketing blueprint.

PART II

BUILDING YOUR BLUEPRINT: THE FOUNDATION, PILLARS, AND OUTCOMES OF AUTHORITY MARKETING

THE FOUNDATION OF AUTHORITY

You Can't Spell Authority Without **AUTHOR**

T he first six letters of the word *Authority* tell us something about the word's relationship to writing and publishing a book. For whatever reason, right or wrong, humans look at authors of books as authorities. An analogy we like to use involves runners. The ultimate achievement in running is to complete a marathon. Lots of people run, and they might run a mile or two a few times a week. They run through their neighborhood, and after those couple miles or so, they're feeling pretty good—but they're beat. To most people the thought of running 26.2 miles seems impossible. That's why when we meet someone who has run a marathon, we're automatically impressed.

Writing and publishing a book is the same thing. You may write every day—many people do, whether it be emails, journaling, or even business-related content. But writing anything more than a thousand words feels like a marathon for most. The thought of writing forty to fifty thousand words seems as impossible as running 26.2 miles. Writing a letter, a blog post, or a few emails is a jog in the park, while writing a book is a marathon.

Because the vast majority of people have never written more than a thousand words at a time, the idea of writing an entire book is a daunting task. You might as well be asking them to scale Mount Everest. And because of the enormity of the task, there's a psychological reaction they have when you introduce yourself as an author. You instantly gain a significant amount of respect because you have accomplished that achievement. Most people don't even need to know what your book is about or have read it. Respect is earned as soon as they hear the words, "I am the author of …"

WRITING A BOOK IS A FORCE-MULTIPLIER. IT ENABLES YOU TO ESTABLISH INSTANT RESPECT AND CREDIBILITY WITH WHOMEVER YOU MEET AND HAVE A CHANCE TO MAKE A LASTING IMPACT.

That's why writing a book is a foundational element of building Authority—a force-multiplier. It enables you to establish instant respect and credibility with whomever you meet and, if a person takes the time to read the book, you also have a chance to make a lasting impact on him or her. Publishing a book makes you an expert on whatever topic your book is on. The perception is that if you have enough knowledge to write a book on a topic, you must know more than most people do about it. We all know a little bit about a lot. But if you know enough about something to write a book on it, people assume you know enough to be *the* Authority on the topic. You're seen as an expert; if you weren't an expert, how could you ever write and publish a book?

Allow us to let you in on a secret about why books are so effective as Authority Marketing tools: it's because they have never been seen as or thought of as marketing tools. Books are scholarly. Books are literary. Books are tools for educating and enlightening ourselves. Nobody thinks of books as a way to sell things, but in reality, they often are. By writing a book, you can market yourself without being seen as a self-promoter. You gain Authority and expert status through a marketing tool which people do not *see* as a marketing tool.

BOOKS ARE SO EFFECTIVE AS AUTHORITY MARKETING TOOLS BECAUSE THEY HAVE NEVER BEEN SEEN AS OR THOUGHT OF AS MARKETING TOOLS.

When you write a book, you might as well tell somebody you're a college professor. You gain a similar level of credibility through Authority by association thanks to centuries and centuries of "authors" being looked to as authorities. Intelligence is one of the many levers that can be pulled to create Authority. Albert Einstein was seen as an Authority, because he was really smart. Stephen Hawking had a name that connoted Authority, because he was viewed as one of the most intelligent people to ever live. When you write a book, people immediately perceive you as someone of high intelligence—because we assume that people who write books are typically very smart. When you write a book, you become the teacher instead of the student.

Authority is completely psychological. When you are perceived as the teacher, that puts others in a mindset where they are ready to learn. This creates a mind shift; when you introduce yourself as an author—especially if it's a topic someone is interested in—you have a chance to make a much bigger impact, because you are speaking to someone who's ready to learn. That means they are going to listen to what you have to say and will likely take your advice. This can be a total game changer, especially if you're selling something; you need people to listen to what you have to say and be willing to take your recommendations. At this point you're prescribing solutions rather than selling products or services, which changes everything.

Another psychological component to authoring a book is the immeasurable value society places on books. We have created permanent shrines for books—from huge libraries down to our own personal bookshelves. We proudly display our books for others to see. As such, we never throw books away. We throw away newspapers and magazines. We TiVo television programs and subscribe to satellite radio so we can consume the media we specifically want, disregard what we don't, and then forget it. Essentially, all other forms of media have become disposable—but not books. Think about it: when was the last time you threw a book away? If you give us a book and we aren't interested in it, we're going to pass it along to someone who is, or else we will donate it to the library. There's a certain guilt that comes with tossing a book into the trash. As a society, humans have come to value books.

ALL OTHER FORMS OF MEDIA HAVE BECOME DISPOSABLE—BUT NOT BOOKS.

The origin of that value we place on books has Judeo-Christian roots. What's the bestselling book of all time? The Bible. The foundation of organized religion as we know it is a book. And the same goes for other faiths; they all have a book at their center. Whether it be the Koran or the Book of Mormon—most faiths are built around a book.

Thus, because many people have a faith-based background, whether or not they practice it today, there is an innate understanding that books are immensely important. It holds true in all cultures that there is a subliminal belief system about the value of books and the Authority of those who write them.

The smartest marketers in the world are better psychologists than they are sales professionals. They understand, at its heart, selling is about persuading, and persuading is emotional and irrational. We buy with emotion—we justify the purchase with logic after the sale.

For all these reasons, the foundational step to become an Authority on a topic—the quickest "affinity" hack that exists—is to author a book on that topic. It pulls all these subconscious psychological triggers and automatically earns you respect, credibility, and trust. It shifts people's mindsets and alters their perceptions of you. We've had people tell us that publishing a book even changed the way their own families look at them! That sounds unbelievable, but it's true. Everyone has the same psychological response—we, the authors of this book, understand the psychology—and we *still* have the same response. That's why we always tell people, if you want to establish and market yourself as an Authority, it starts with authoring a book.

WHAT DO I WRITE ABOUT?

Before you can figure out *what* you should write about, you have to ask yourself why you're writing a book. There are a lot of reasons why someone might want to write a book, and they're all valid in their own right.

Many dentists have found that books can help elevate their practice above others in their area in terms of new patient intake. A book can be a tool to showcase expertise in the field, inform an audience, and attract more patients. Some people are motivated by legacy. It's a matter of them wanting to have some say in how they're remembered. *What are my grandkids and great-grandkids going to know about me? What are the employees of my company going to know about me fifty years after I am gone?* Legacy is significant, and it's a good reason to write a book. Books often cement legacy.

Education or impact is another reason. Most authorities aren't just trying to grow their business or make money; they have a true desire to make an impact by educating others and helping them make better decisions. Knowledge is power, and people are moved to share their knowledge with the world. By doing so, they can help people to become more informed and have an impact on the world. Which, of course, is another excellent reason to write a book.

For some, writing a book is a bucket-list item. There's nothing wrong with that. In fact, according to *The Huffington Post*, over 80 percent of Americans want to write a book before they die. Only a miniscule fraction of those people actually will, but it is a widespread desire.

Many people who want to write do it for entertainment. They want to entertain others and craft compelling stories. We all love a good story, and many works of fiction have become very influential.

However, if you're reading this book, we suspect the main reason you would want to write a book would be to grow your practice and make a larger impact by creating Authority for yourself and your company. By establishing yourself as a thought leader, you make your practice and yourself a magnet for opportunity. That doesn't mean your book can't accomplish multiple goals—it can definitely educate people about what you do or the field you work in, and it can serve as a legacy builder. But along the way we want the book to open doors for you to reach a much larger group of people.

With practice growth and broader impact in mind, the best advice when it comes to deciding what to write about is to bait the hook to suit the fish, not the fisherman. Many authors make this mistake. They write the book that they want to write and then hope there's an audience that cares enough to read it. Instead, authors should ask, "What is the yearning, burning problem that my target patient is grappling with?" Then write a book that addresses that.

If you want to write a book that will serve as the ultimate marketing tool, then you have to write about a topic that the people who have the ability and willingness to buy from you care about. If you can address the problems that your prospective customer or patient is facing, all the better. No matter what it is, what you write about has to be of importance to people who have the capacity and ultimately the desire to give your business money. What we mean by that is, a lot of people write a book for the masses. When you ask them who their target reader is they'll say, "Everybody! Everybody should read my book. There's not a single person who wouldn't benefit."

The truth is, if you're writing for everybody, you're really writing for nobody. With more than 320 million people in America, and more than 7 billion worldwide, there is no way your book is ever going to achieve any significant penetration in such a target market.

As a marketer, it is financially impractical to reach a widespread global audience; you have to have a bull's-eye mentality when you write a book. Sure, it may benefit anyone who reads it, but if you want an efficient and effective journey to becoming an Authority, you want to have a very clear idea of who will benefit most.

HOW DO I GET MY BOOK WRITTEN?

There's a reason why, even though over 80 percent of people say they want to write a book, less than a fraction of 1 percent ever do. It's not because they aren't good writers—in fact, many good writers never complete a book. It isn't because they're not passionate about it, either. The plain and simple fact is writing a book takes a lot of time. Most people don't have time to write a book, just as most people don't have the time it takes to train to run a marathon. The commitment that a task of such enormity requires is downright overwhelming—to the point where it's paralyzing for many.

There's a sign hanging at our office in Charleston, South Carolina, that reads, "How Do You Eat an Elephant?" The answer, of course, is "one bite at a time." The journey of a thousand miles begins with one step. The same is true of writing a book. It's just a matter of figuring out what that first step should be for you.

So how do you write your book? Well, the first answer to that question is this: maybe you shouldn't. What we mean is, maybe you shouldn't write the book yourself. There's a difference between authoring a book and writing a book. Writing a book is sitting down at a computer and typing each line *yourself*—letting the words flow from your mind through the keyboard or onto the page. For many people, this is really, really hard.

One reason people find this so difficult is that we live incredibly distracted, fast-paced lives in a world that doesn't allow for much undivided attention. Everything today is microbursts and microseconds, as opposed to long periods of uninterrupted quiet. There are mobile devices, instant-news alerts, and a myriad of other distractions that we all deal with on top of our day-to-day responsibilities.

Another reason writing a book proves difficult is that most people are better at verbalizing ideas than they are at writing them down. They can easily share their stories, passion, and knowledge verbally, but the task of writing them down and organizing them into paragraphs and chapters is unfamiliar and unnatural. Doing that requires a specific skill set that many people haven't learned. That's why you might want to consider working with someone who has experience doing that and can help you through the process.

However, just because you may not actually write a book doesn't mean you aren't authoring it. The author of the book is the one who has the ideas and knowledge to share. A book is written in the author's voice. He or she is the one who ultimately decides what is included and how it is approached. A writer can help the author to organize his or her ideas and get them onto the page. The author is the *Authority*—a writer can be utilized to help bring the vision to life.

THE AUTHOR IS THE *AUTHORITY*— A WRITER CAN BE UTILIZED TO HELP BRING THE VISION TO LIFE.

If you choose not to write a book yourself, there are some options. You can work with a company like ours—Advantage|Business

Journals Books|ForbesBooks—which allows you to *talk* through your book with a professional writer, or you can have a professional ghostwriter assigned to you directly. In either scenario, you're working closely with someone who will help you turn your vision, experience, and knowledge into a book. We can tell you from personal experience that this is a very common method used by health and dental professionals to create their books. It takes on average more than three years for a businessperson to write his or her own book. As mentioned earlier, a lot of that is due to interruptions and time constraints. By contrast, working with a third party to create your book enables you to finish the process in as little as six months.

If you do choose to write your own book—as *we*, Adam and Rusty, each have in the past—you will have to regard it as a commitment. It is going to take discipline and regimentation. You need to begin with the end in mind—what is it going to look like? What is it going to accomplish? Who's your target reader? What problems are you addressing for them? With those questions, you craft a blueprint for your book, and then you schedule time on your calendar to work on it. Block off the period of time each day that you are most productive. For some, that's early in the morning. For others, it might be the afternoon or evening. Figure out when your golden hours are—the times when you are at your best—and schedule time to write. The real trick is sticking to it.

HOW DO I PUBLISH MY BOOK?

When you finally have your book complete, what do you do with it? The good news is that it has never been easier to get a book published. The not-so-good news is, because it's never been easier, it's never been more important that the book be done *correctly*. Many years ago, you could have cut corners and most readers might not have noticed the difference—just having a book was itself enough to establish you as an Authority.

Think of it this way: if you're living in a small town, you may be the best singer there. You might have a reputation among all the locals for having a great voice. But if you were to move to Nashville or Austin, where everybody is singing at a professional level, you might discover you weren't as good as you had assumed. The same thing goes for writing a book. When nobody was publishing books, you could write a book that was a six or seven out of ten on the quality scale and you would be okay. But now that it's become so easy to publish, you have to be a ten out of ten in quality to stand out.

NOW THAT IT'S BECOME SO EASY TO PUBLISH, YOU HAVE TO BE A TEN OUT OF TEN IN QUALITY TO STAND OUT.

Once you have your book, and you're confident it's a ten, there are three avenues you can take when it comes to publishing. You can self-publish, find a traditional publisher, or invest in hybrid publishing.

Self-publishing is pretty simple; you do it all yourself. That means you reap all the benefits and maintain full control of the project. That also means you have to figure everything out on your own. The big problem with self-publishing is that 90 percent of books that are self-published *look* like they're self-published. If you hear someone say, "This book looks like it was self-published," that's not a good thing. Although we're told not to judge a book by its cover, the truth is every book's first impression is made by its cover. (Remember phase one of branding!)

That means your book has to look as good and read as well as any you would find on the front table at Barnes & Noble. This is a must! It's not a matter of "it would be nice if it looked professional." It *has* to look the part. If your book is not every bit as good as those you find at the retail book stores, don't publish it! If the image your book creates in the minds of your audience is not congruent with the quality you provide, *it will do you more harm than good.*

The other side of the coin is traditional publishing, which is how Rusty published his first book, and he had a great experience with it. For some people this is a good fit. If you're already a well-known person, or have a widely known brand, traditional publishing may be the route you want to take. Likewise, if you're already a published author, you know your project is going to get attention, and therefore, it makes sense to continue using traditional publishers.

Unfortunately, in today's publishing landscape, that may not be a realistic option for most people, as there are fewer and fewer traditional publishers and most are raising the bar on what they will accept. All authors dream of getting agents who will go out and get them $100,000 advances on their books. They'll get published, the publisher will promote and market the book, and they'll get rich. Then all they have to do is sit back and collect royalty checks. That's pure fantasy. For most people, it just doesn't happen.

In fact, the majority of the titles that appear on the *New York Times* nonfiction bestseller list each year are those written by authors who had previously already had a bestselling book. The odds are stacked against you when it comes to breaking into that pool. It comes down to haves and have-nots. The ones who get the big contracts are often those who already have big names and an established track record in their brands and platforms.

Even if you do manage to get through the gates, there are three realities to be aware of with traditional publishing:

1. First, it takes an average of twelve to eighteen months to get published. That means you must have lots of patience—as well as a message that isn't incredibly time-sensitive.

2. Second, the publisher owns the rights to the book, which can put handcuffs on you in regard to what you can and can't do with the book.

3. Finally, you need to consider how much your publisher is going to do. They will get it into bookstores, perhaps, but they're likely going to rely on *you* to do most of the marketing. The books aren't going to sell themselves, and, outside of unique cases, a traditional publisher isn't going to put a lot of money into promoting them for you. In fact, your ability to promote the book to your platform is probably one of the reasons they bought the book from you!

We work with a lot of traditional publishers and most do fantastic work, including the publisher of Rusty's first book, but it's important to be aware that traditional publishing isn't a fit for everyone.

The third route is hybrid publishing. That's where you engage a company that specializes in publishing and marketing your book. You hire them to create and publish a book that looks as good and reads as well as any you find on the shelves at Barnes & Noble. Then, when that is done, you have a partner that can help you make money using the book to grow your business. That's the goal most professionals have when they publish a book. To do it, you want a partner that has experience working with dentists and health professionals to establish and market their Authority status.

THE GOAL MOST PROFESSIONALS HAVE WHEN THEY PUBLISH A BOOK IS TO GROW THEIR BUSINESS.

If you go this route, however, you have to understand the aim of hybrid publishing is not to sell books. While some individuals will be able to have successful sales, the majority of authors who go this route will not. If you are interviewing a hybrid publisher and they are promising huge sales or leading you to that conclusion, you may want to reconsider that relationship. That doesn't mean you *won't* make money on the book—you can, just not in the way most people envision when they think of writing a book. The best hybrid publishers understand that, for authorities, there are far better ways to make money with a book than by selling it. Good ones teach you how to use your book as a marketing tool—how to use the Authority it gives you to grow your business. The book serves as the foundation from which you can leverage media and generate leads. With the right direction, doing this can give you an immeasurable advantage over your competitors. If done right, creating a book is an investment with exponential returns—but you have to go in with your eyes wide open on the outcome you are seeking.

THE PILLARS OF AUTHORITY

ow that you know what Authority Marketing is and understand why it is so important to establish trust that allows you to get your message out/amplify your message in the new media landscape, and understand how a book is the foundation, we are going to dive deep together on the four foundational pillars that build Authority.

1. **Branding and Omnipresence**

2. **Content Marketing**

3. **PR & Media**

4. **Speaking**

Most leaders generally accept that thought leadership is important but few know how to actually do that. This section will provide that roadmap, diving deep into each pillar and describing how you can use each to establish and grow your Authority. We will also closely examine the importance of cultivating an online brand presence—and the equally important task of consistently conducting an Authority Marketing Audit to ensure its maximum effectiveness! An Authority

Marketing Audit allows you to get a clear view of where you stand on each Authority Marketing pillar so you know which areas need improvement. Once it's complete, you have a clear idea which areas to focus resources and attention on as you continue to build your Authority.

Branding and Omnipresence

Many people reading this book are dentists or practice partners who have been focusing on building their practice's brand and reputation for years. However, in large part, they have neglected their personal brand—what we think of as their *Authority brand*.

Have you ever thought of yourself as a brand?

We—the authors—often get an initial recoil from audiences when we ask that question. To some it feels awkward and maybe even a bit egotistical to think of themselves as a brand. And, sure—we get it—there are plenty of examples out there of personal brands gone wrong, often falling victim to over-promotitis.

But, as we have discussed, that initial recoil shouldn't prevent you from taking yourself—and your brand—seriously, as the quality, visibility, and differentiation of that brand will determine many opportunities in the future.

Many are surprised by the importance of their personal brand. Some have just "never thought about it" and have created successful careers through interpersonal relationships and good work. At the same time, many of our fellow business and practice leaders understand the importance of branding but focus entirely on their corporate brand as opposed to their own personal brand's Authority.

It is very important to build a corporate brand, but it's also expensive, time-consuming, and just plain hard to do in today's media landscape. There are several reasons why:

❑ **Power to the people |** We are more drawn to individuals than corporations in the current business climate. We simply trust people more than generic businesses. (See J.J. Watt's successful Hurricane Harvey fundraiser vs. nonprofit brand fundraisers as just one recent example.)

❑ **David vs. Goliath |** Corporate brands are often competing against other corporations who have been around for decades and have many millions more to spend on branding, making it much harder to stand out. (When you compete as a thought leader/Authority, you level the playing field.)

❑ **Thought leadership vs. advertising |** When it comes to speaking, media coverage, and event opportunities, businesses are seen as advertisers/sponsors who sell, and individuals are perceived as thought leaders/Authorities who provide value.

Understanding that your personal brand is your secret weapon, where should you start?

Understand What Branding Is

If we were to ask the first thousand people who read this book what the definition of branding is, we would probably get a thousand different answers. It's an overused and often misunderstood term.

Yet the definition of branding is simple—*creating an image in the mind of your audience.*

Think about it: a "brand" is something that creates an image in your mind. Businesses or people you've never heard of don't have a brand with you; no image is created in your mind. On the other hand, consider some of these well-known brands: United Airlines, Hertz, Marriott, Four Seasons, or Authority brands like Suze Orman, Oprah Winfrey, or Dave Ramsey. Likely, an image comes to mind for each of these; they have built a "brand." What does building a brand look like in the world of dentistry?

DR. R. CRAIG MILLER

Nearly a decade ago, Dr. R. Craig Miller began writing his manuscript for a book that was meant to showcase his extensive knowledge in the dental field. He shelved it, however, after life and work got in the way. In 2017, Dr. Miller was encouraged by a colleague to write about his vast expertise in the industry. "You're knowledgeable, and you're a good storyteller. Why don't you write a book?" His colleague's encouraging prodding gave him the motivation he needed to try again. Dr. Miller revisited, revised, and finished his manuscript with Advantage. The result? Much more than a book. Dr. Miller has effectively implemented powerful personal and professional branding efforts that have positively affected his career and his outlook.

Since the publication of *Get Back Your Smile, Take Back Your Life*, Dr. Miller's networking and branding opportunities have skyrocketed. Not only has his credibility with his peers improved, but the image of Authority that his authorship imparts has led to marketing and media engagement opportunities. This ranges from speaking engagements, where slides featuring *Get Back Your Smile* bookend his presentations, to The Miller Center's website, where highlighting the book helps establish the credibility that grounds the fresh and relevant content Dr. Miller promotes. "Being a published author certainly brings a powerful punch to any efforts in media and all its outlets," Dr. Miller notes.

The image that's conjured in the mind of Dr. Miller's coliseum audience is that of someone who "knows their stuff"—someone whose expertise and didacticism led them to becoming a published author. It's already impressive that Dr. Miller is one of his region's top dentists, but the circulation of his book takes that impression a step further: it marks him as a nationwide expert. "The book brands me as one of the top 1-2 percent of dentists in the country," Dr. Miller explains. Branding his practice is nearly effortless when his personal brand already carries such Authority.

In 2020, Dr. Miller was named one of New Jersey's top doctors. This, combined with the phrase "published author," is enough to capture anyone's attention and bring forth the image every Authority wants their name and credentials to conjure. "Anything after 'published author' has more weight. It holds the reader longer," Dr. Miller observes.

But it's not just about branding for business's sake, though. Publication, and the increased credibility that comes with it, has made it more possible than ever for Dr. Miller to share his knowledge. "The credibility factor in authorship keeps me closer to the pulse of the field," he tells us. He is that much more likely to be the speaker chosen for an upcoming engagement, to be the dentist chosen for an interview, or to be the person at the front of another doctor's mind when they're making a referral. This means, ultimately, that Dr. Miller is able to help more patients. And with his rigorous schedule of continued education—averaging around a hundred to two hundred hours of study a year, compared with New Jersey's required twenty hours—it's clear that Dr. Miller knows his stuff.

Because his brand successfully marks him as an Authority, Dr. Miller gets to concentrate on what's important to him: his passion for the profession he loves.

Although many people think of branding as a logo, or the way their product looks (and yes, that's certainly part of it), branding is really about the image that comes to mind when someone thinks of a corporation, nonprofit, or person—whatever that image may be.

Do you know what image comes to the mind of your audience when your name is mentioned? Hopefully it's one that evokes feelings of trust, affinity, and likeability. An image created as a result of your audience getting to know you or buying your product or service.

But what about those people who have never heard of you before? How can you build a brand with them in the age of digital first impressions?

To be successful at building an Authority brand, you must understand that there are two phases to branding (creating an image in your audience's mind).

PHASE-ONE IMAGE (AND YOUR BRAND AUDIT)

The first phase is what a patient sees prior to any direct interaction with you, your team, or your product/services. You don't yet have a "brand" with this person because no image comes to his or her mind. In this phase, your brand is what Google says it is—cementing an initial image without any direct interaction from you.

Does that make you nervous? For many readers of this book, it should, as this phase-one image often starts on page one of Google and, for many, it ends there—especially if you aren't discoverable via a Google search on your name.

However, when you own search on your name and have created a phase-one image that clearly presents you as a standout Authority with a differentiated, mission-driven message, that image encourages a client or patient to take the next step and learn more. On the other hand, if a search presents a bad, confusing, or even nonexistent image, you will miss out on him or her taking that next step.

Having a nonexistent, confusing, or negative phase-one image makes it almost impossible to track how many leads or opportunities you may have lost at this phase—because you never hear from those potential patients, journalists, or possible referral sources who Googled you. There are other factors, as well, which we will walk through later in the book, but it's important to understand that *this is the phase where Authority Marketing really gives you an opportunity to differentiate your brand from others.*

So, where should you start in terms of better understanding the phase-one impression you're creating?

Imagine that a business associate had dinner with a *Wall Street Journal* reporter last night, and over the course of the dinner, the reporter indicated he or she needed to talk to an expert in your field for a story. Score! Your colleague gladly writes your name on a napkin but doesn't have your email address or contact information at the time. When that reporter has a chance to Google you, can you be found? Specifically, are there results on page one that connect back to you? Do you own any of those results? Is it your website or a blog? Is it your social-media channel? Is it an online review site?

There is a key difference between "owning" a search (your website/blog) and being found on results that others own.

Imagine, for example, that you are a physician who hasn't been intentional about building an online brand. When somebody Googles your name, a website like Healthgrades is likely the number one result that comes up. That means *you* don't own your first impression—Healthgrades does. So, the first impression someone gets of your brand—which we have already discussed is *the* most important impression—is owned by somebody else. Someone other than you is controlling how that first impression is made.

Which leads us to the concept of the *online brand audit*—the extremely important section of your Authority blueprint that involves finding out if you can be found when that *Wall Street Journal* reporter searches for you. And considering the impression being made when you are found.

Let's say the top result in a Google search for your name is your website—awesome! Well, hopefully awesome. When patients click through to your website, will what they find encourage them or dissuade them from reaching out to you? Are they going to say, "Yes, this is the thought leader I am looking for"? Do they get the impression that you are the go-to Authority, or has your website not been updated in three years? Are they finding something on YouTube, perhaps an old TV interview you gave or a bad review, that leads them to question your Authority?

When you're conducting a brand audit, one of the things you really want to consider is which results you own and which you do not. Things like online reviews, old videos, and so on often live on online real estate that you don't own. As you review the results, ask yourself this question: "Is there anything online that will detract from that first impression, and if so, how can I deal with it as quickly as possible?"

"IS THERE ANYTHING ONLINE THAT WILL DETRACT FROM THAT FIRST IMPRESSION, AND IF SO, HOW CAN I DEAL WITH IT AS QUICKLY AS POSSIBLE?"

Nobody is perfect. It is not uncommon, when we at Advantage|Business Journals Books|ForbesBooks are conducting a brand audit for a Member, to find things that could be detractors when it comes to making the initial impression. Maybe there's a bad review, or somebody wrote something unflattering about you or your practice. It may be something unfair, but it's there for anyone searching your name to see. The key thing to do when that happens is to (A) respond to the bad review with empathy and a next step that brings it to a resolution and (B) focus on outranking it—getting positive results to place above any detracting results.

Own Your Online Real Estate

Often, the best way to "outrank" results you don't own on a search for your name is to *own* your name as a website.

This is one of the first things we want to encourage you to do as you read this book! If you don't own your name as a URL (firstnamelastname.com, or if you're a doctor, drfirstnamelastname.com), put down the book right now, head over to GoDaddy.com or another online registrar service, and purchase your name as a website address. While you're at it, reserve the name of your kids (or even grandkids). Online real estate is highly valuable today—and it is only going to get more valuable in the future. Owning that real estate is one of the first steps to owning the first impression people get when they Google your name.

Most executives have a presence on their corporate websites, but when building Authority, you also want to have a personal brand, or as we call it, an Authority-brand website. This will be your home base online as a mission-driven thought leader, speaker, and even author. This is a website which is focused on three things:

1. **Visually showcasing Authority-building accomplishments:** Media interviews you've given in the past, speaking engagements you've had, any books you may have written, and even brands you have worked with. If you don't have a large brand yet, Authority is built best by association with other brands that people *do* know. Do this visually within your website.

2. **Sharing the mission behind your work:** You want a home base that builds the perception that you aren't just an expert, but an author, a media personality, a keynote speaker, or a philanthropist who is intent on making an impact with your message.

3.   **Providing value to your audience:** A modern website is much more than an online brochure (more on this later in this section)—it's an online-media property that provides fresh content to inform and entertain your audience.

A standalone website, with your name as the URL, not only gives you a great chance to own your first impression, but it makes the kind of impression that really adds to your Authority.

Should You Change Your Name?

Another thing to consider when it comes to your online brand audit is the commonality of your name. Be honest with yourself about this. Do you have a common name? If your name is John Smith or Bill Miller, or something else that is shared by lots of people all over the world, the chances of you owning that first impression on Google searches are slim. Likewise, if you share a name with a celebrity, like Brad Pitt or Michael Jackson, or anyone else who is so far out front in terms of Authority or visibility, you need to pause and think about the possibility of changing your name. Of course, that doesn't mean getting your first or last name legally changed, but if you want to "own" your name as a brand online, you're likely going to need to add your middle name or a middle initial to your name. That subtle addition could be a game changer in terms of establishing a unique brand and owning your online presence.

Consider bestselling author David Meerman Scott, one of the leading authorities in PR and marketing. For many years his name was David Scott, but he made the decision early in his career that he was never going to be able to fully own that brand online. David Scott was just too common a name. By adding his middle name, he has been able to establish and own his own brand. He uses that name consistently across his Authority Marketing efforts.

That brings us to brand consistency. If you add your middle name to your brand, you should consistently use that anywhere your name appears. Your Twitter handle, your Facebook URL, your LinkedIn, your business cards, how you're introduced at speaking events, how TV hosts introduce you. Everything! Consistency across all media platforms and anywhere your name appears is crucial for building your brand. Using different names creates confusion and hinders your ability to build equity in that brand.

Now we've covered discoverability when someone knows to look for you by name. Next, we get into the real, *significant* Authority that determines how easily people who have never even heard of you can find you. For example, if customers are looking for a great financial advisor in Phoenix, or a top Realtor in Baton Rouge, or a keynote speaker on the changing realities of marketing, will your name appear on an indirect search on your topic area or field?

When you start being discoverable in indirect searches like these, that's when you will really start pulling in more of a significant Authority platform. As we continue to go through this section, we're going to talk to you about how to widen your net around indirect searches. But the first level of this, again, is to perform an online brand audit, search your own name, topic of Authority, or field and see where you currently place in the results. That's the foundation— the first thing you should focus on.

PHASE-TWO IMAGE

The second phase of branding is the image that is created as a direct result of interacting with you, whether it is reading your book, hearing you give a speech, meeting you in person, or becoming a patient at your practice.

The image that is created in this phase directly relates back to whether we underdeliver or overdeliver on the impression. In other words, think about well-known brands like Delta Airlines, Uber, or the Four Seasons. The image that comes to your mind related to those brands connects back to the totality of your experience doing business with them. If you're a happy customer, a positive phase-two image comes to mind and you're likely to refer friends to that company. If a company underdelivers, you have a negative brand image in your mind and may even become a detractor.

Many of the entrepreneurs we speak with have 80–90 percent of their lead flow coming from referrals and word of mouth, which is the sign of a great phase-two business. Although this tells us we're sitting in front of someone who runs a great operational business, often these same owners are frustrated with the slow growth rate—something I'm sure a lot of you reading this book can relate to. But the limiting factor of a business that relies primarily on phase two (meaning the owner or business doesn't focus on building Authority, owning search, or driving third-party credibility) for leads is that the business doesn't have any direct control over promotion. It has indirect control—do a great job for customers and they will drive referrals—but in this situation you are totally beholden to others taking action to drive leads and grow your business. This is a helpless feeling for an entrepreneur or leader, but it is the reality for many dentists who find themselves a commoditized option competing with many others to win over patients—even when they do great work!

We encourage you to think about your brand across both phases and be intentional about *discoverability*, Authority by association, and mission-driven positioning to create the best possible image in the minds of your audience.

Content Marketing

The first step toward a successful content marketing strategy is taking a step back to look at the changing media landscape. Without this big-picture view, you end up where most people do on the content marketing front—working really hard, spending lots of money and not getting any traction.

To Rent, to Earn, or to Own?

The third era of Authority Marketing is the fastest-moving era because we are marketing in an environment that is changing much quicker than either of the first two ever did thanks to the speed of technology.

The reason traditional media drove Authority in the second era is because they had a total monopoly on information distribution. During those hundred or so years, there were really only two ways to get a message out at scale: you could either rent the media's platform by buying an ad (rented media) or you could earn your way onto their platform (earned media) by getting an interview or speaking engagement.

But there was no way to go around the media to reach an audience directly at scale—people had to go through major media to do it. As such, large companies with big budgets had all the power in the second era, because smaller companies or individuals couldn't afford to build Authority or give themselves leverage in their market by owning the connection to their audience. In other words, outside of amassing a physical mailing list, which was hard and cumbersome to build and expensive to reach consistently, you couldn't "be the media"—you had to go through them.

Fast forward to our current era: we still have rented and earned media, but the biggest game changer in the third era of Authority Marketing is the growth of owned media.

Before going further, let's take a more in-depth look at the three categories of media in the new media landscape, a framework initially put forth in *Mastering the New Media Landscape: Embrace the Micromedia Mindset* (Berrett-Koehler, 2016), which Rusty coauthored with Barbara Cave Henricks:

❑ **Rented Media:** This includes all media where you fully control the content but you don't own the real estate— including advertising, social media channels (your LinkedIn account, Facebook page, etc.), bio pages on provider sites, and so on. Rented media doesn't provide much Authority because the audience knows the barrier to entry is incredibly low: after all, anyone can buy an ad or start a Twitter account. Plus, it doesn't provide targeted access to your audience at scale and on a road back to your owned media—where, for the purposes of Authority Marketing, all roads should lead!

❑ **Earned Media:** This includes all media on real estate you don't own where the perception of the audience is that you *earned* the media—including publicity, speaking engagements, online reviews, referrals, word-of-mouth, your book, and beyond. Nothing provides more immediate Authority than earned media, and, as a result, many people make the mistake of putting all their eggs in this single basket, which is very dangerous, because you don't have direct control over media going out. Think about it; with earned media you have to rely on someone else to do something for a message to go out (e.g., your patient has to be at the right dinner party next to the right person to make that referral; the producer has to say yes to putting you on air, etc.).

❑ **Owned Media:** This includes any asset where you fully own the connection to your audience, providing you with more leverage than any other category of media, because you own the real estate. Your website, blog, email list, and even a physical mailing list all live within this category.

Each of these three organically feed each other, but when you consider owned media in the context of the new media landscape, success comes when you intentionally focus on moving your audience from rented and earned media to your owned media. Unfortunately, most leaders, companies, and brands still have online platforms built for that previous media environment—and it's costing them dearly.

What do we mean?

As we have mentioned, success today means thinking more like the media than a marketer. Media outlets are focused on attention and, more specifically, doing everything they can to earn and then own the attention from their audience on an ongoing basis.

We want you to do the exact same thing.

SUCCESS TODAY MEANS THINKING MORE LIKE THE MEDIA THAN A MARKETER. MEDIA OUTLETS ARE FOCUSED ON ATTENTION.

ADOPT A MEDIA MINDSET TO FILL YOUR COLISEUM

To take a more intentional approach to patient generation, it's important to understand that you have three audiences in place at all times. To explain this framework in more detail, we're going to look to the world of sports.

We want you to visualize your owned-media audience as a coliseum that belongs to you. Coauthor Adam is thinking about Memorial Stadium or "Death Valley," as it's also known, in Clemson. Your other coauthor, Rusty, is thinking about Darrell K. Royal–Texas Memorial Stadium in Austin. We'll defer to each reader to pick whichever stadium/coliseum comes to mind based on your own background and, at the behest of our editors, we'll leave the argument over which is the best sports venue for another day.

Close your eyes and visualize your 360-degree coliseum with a stage in the middle and an inner ring of VIP seats around the stage. This inner ring of VIP seats is your **Customer Audience.** The outer ring of seats is your **Attention Audience.** People that are not inside the coliseum, walking around outside, are your **Target Audience.**

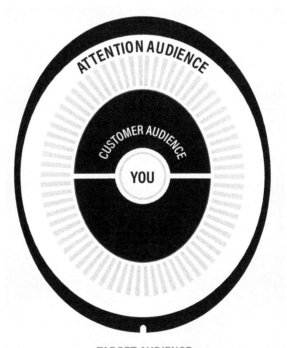

❑ **Customer Audience:** This includes your existing patients and strategic partners—everyone who is spending money with you. They are seated close to the stage in the VIP section. How many do you have in your Customer Audience?

❑ **Attention Audience:** This group sits in the outer ring of seats and includes everyone on your email list or snail-mail list who has not yet decided to spend money with you. They are paying attention—but you haven't established enough affinity with them to move them backstage with a purchase. How many people do you have in your Attention Audience?

❑ **Target Audience:** This group is outside your coliseum and includes everyone who has no idea who you are but could benefit from your products, services, or message.

Most marketing and advertising campaigns focus on reaching as many Target Audience people as possible and trying to immediately convert them to your Customer Audience—folks who will buy something from you or sign up for some high-touch appointment like a free consultation. The reality in today's skeptical landscape is that few people are ready after the very first brand impression to take that large a jump the first time they hear about you—which means that marketing and advertising campaigns that drive people to this kind of call to action provide much less value than they should. When you reach people in your Target Audience there are basically three things that can happen:

1. A tiny percentage are ready to come to you as a patient immediately (less than 1 percent on most campaigns).

2.   A small percentage are intrigued and want to learn more but aren't yet sure if you're the right person/product/service for their need.

3.   A large percentage have no interest whatsoever.

When you have a marketing mindset with your promotion, you are only set up to convert the first category: people ready to become a patient now. That kind of approach focuses on generating impressions and turning them into immediate patients or inquiries for more information, which only provides value to the tiny percentage of people who are immediately looking for a new dentist in the area, or want to switch providers based on an insurance change or bad experience with their former provider.

We can't overstate the importance of understanding the shift that has taken place and the opportunity it provides to you as someone who wants to grow your visibility, impact, and bottom line.

For years, marketing has been about immediate conversions. X number of brochures led to Y number of calls. X number of cold calls led to Y number of leads. X spent on advertising led to Y ROI. But the limiting factor on these "traditional" lead-generation tactics is that they only allowed you to convert those people who you happened to get lucky enough to reach on the right day when they were ready to buy—you had no opportunity to nurture that additional group of people you reached who were interested in your topic area but weren't ready to convert that day. As such, you got a fraction of the value from the money and time you spent on lead-generation efforts.

By contrast, a media mindset focuses also (not instead; you're still converting those ready to buy) on extending the interaction with your Attention Audience by providing a mutually beneficial way for them to get value and learn more—giving you a chance to nurture that contact and build affinity over time, moving them down toward the stage to head into the VIP section with fellow patients.

The Three-Step Purchase Process

The three-step affinity process in today's media landscape is as follows: awareness, attention, and affinity. Each is accelerated with Authority.

THE THREE-STEP PURCHASE PROCESS IN TODAY'S MEDIA LANDSCAPE IS AS FOLLOWS: AWARENESS, ATTENTION, AND AFFINITY. EACH IS ACCELERATED WITH AUTHORITY.

Awareness happens when you first make an impression on someone. Based on that first phase of branding—the image you created in their minds once they became aware of you—and their broader interest in your topic area, you have the potential to move them to the next phase where they give you their attention. (Figuratively speaking, they just took a seat in your Attention Audience in your coliseum). Once you have their attention, you have the opportunity to build affinity with them over time.

Let's translate this important analogy into a more practical application.

When someone lands on your website, he or she is walking into your coliseum. Imagine that person peering down from the rafters with one question in mind: "Is there anything valuable for me to do here?"

Think about your website, provided you have one: does it more closely resemble an online brochure or a media property?

Ninety-nine percent of the websites we look at are nothing more than digital brochures—they provide information on the company or individual, including "about-us" content, location, services offered, and contact information. Some might even offer a free consultation or appointment. There's not much difference between that kind of website and a print brochure.

Think about the last brochure you were handed. You might have glanced through it and maybe the design even impressed you, but if you weren't ready to act on the information provided at that precise moment, you likely tossed it in the trash and forgot about it.

Similarly, if your website is set up like an online brochure, you're only converting the tiny percentage of site visitors who happen to reach your website at the precise moment they are ready to buy or contact you. All the other visitors are going to close the tab on their internet browser or hit the back button—essentially chunking your website aside, just like they would a brochure.

This kind of approach—consistent with a marketing mindset— is the reason why most advertising, PR, and marketing budgets go up almost entirely in smoke. You might have the best PR firm ever or be driving a huge number of clicks from that Facebook advertising campaign, and people are basically flooding into your coliseum! BUT if you have a website set up like an online brochure, where the only call to action is either to buy or "contact us" for more information or a free appointment, it's pretty much the same as asking them to walk all the way down from the rafters to the stage the first time they arrive. That means that you're only set up to convert the tiny sub 1 percent of people who land on your website who are immediately ready to buy something or take action.

Far too many people spend a fortune on rented media ad campaigns or earned-media high-end PR firms that drive a ton of traffic back to their coliseum—but the crucial miss is that it's a revolving door. Instead of asking someone to walk all the way down to the stage, money in hand, and jump from your Target Audience to your Customer Audience the first time they arrive, we want to encourage you to shift your strategy and give them a reason to take a seat in your Attention Audience.

Reaching into Other Coliseums

Many of you may be thinking, "This makes a lot of sense, but I don't have very many people in my coliseum just yet, that's why I'm reading this book!" We get it—and the framework we've just established with your owned-media coliseum informs the next step: going into other coliseums to drive people back to yours.

Any time you run a marketing or promotional campaign, whether it is a Facebook ad campaign, a radio advertisement, an NPR interview, or a speaking engagement, you reach an indirect audience in real estate that others own (whether rented or earned). When you do this, you're essentially standing on the stage in a coliseum that they own. This is true of any piece of rented or earned media. For example, if you write an article for Forbes.com, imagine you are standing on stage in a very big coliseum that Forbes owns, one that is filled to the rafters with tens of millions of unique monthly visitors. It may be hard to believe, but they have given you a small sliver of their stage when they publish your article. Your goal with that article is twofold:

1. To deliver great content.

2. To give as many people as possible who read that article a reason to get up out of their seat in that Forbes stadium

and follow you out the door to your stadium—in effect, driving them to your website.

When giving a speech, doing an interview, or writing an article, most people focus only on the first goal—to give great content. Obviously, you must do that, but it doesn't end there. If you do what most people do, which is feature a bio that encourages people to "learn more" on their website, you may get lucky and have a few people follow you out the door of Forbes's coliseum, but most people won't leave their seats.

You have probably long since caught on that we wrote this book because we don't want you to do what most people do. Instead, we want you to offer that audience in the Forbes coliseum a clear, value-packed reason to get up out of their seat and follow you out the door to *your* coliseum—your website! This is called a *lead magnet*, and those who have already embraced the micromedia mindset have been using them for years to grow an "owned-media" subscriber base.

Lead magnets come in many shapes and sizes, but we like to organize them into two big picture buckets:

- **The Target→Attention lead magnet:** taking someone from your Target Audience (having never heard of you before) to your Attention Audience (joining your email list). This is the lead magnet we want you to use in a rented or earned media environment.

- **The Attention→Customer lead magnet:** taking someone from your email list (Attention Audience) to buying something from you (Customer Audience). This is the lead magnet that is woven into content marketing—working people toward a purchase.

Although it may sound counterintuitive, the harder lead magnet is the Target→Attention conversion—taking someone from having never heard of you to joining your email list. There are three categories of Target→Attention lead magnets:

1. **Newsletter sign-up:** The first is the most basic and, unfortunately, the most commonly used. This often shows up as "click here to join our email newsletter" or "click here to sign up for exclusive news and updates." As you might guess, or as you already know if this is your current lead magnet, this call to action converts at a horrific rate.

2. **Free-value offer:** The second category typically shows up in one of the following ways: "Click here to download our whitepaper/e-book/workbook," or "Click here for a free consultation" etc. This category converts better than the first one, but the limiting factor for those who don't yet have a brand established is that those who are landing on your website for the first time may not associate value with your content yet, which limits conversions.

3. **Interactive content:** The third category is the one we, the authors, want you to shift to. Interactive content includes quizzes and assessments that give free, personalized value to website visitors. Magazines have been using quizzes for years, but BuzzFeed was the first online platform to really perfect the art of online interactive content. Books like Tom Rath's *StrengthsFinder 2.0*, Sally Hogshead's *How the World Sees You*, and Katty Kay and Claire Shipman's *The Confidence Code* leveraged high-value assessments to build email lists in the hundreds of thousands.

The magic of good quiz/assessment marketing is that it is the purest possible value exchange; *both* parties get value. Your website visitor gets free, personalized feedback based on the topic of the quiz. They might learn what your practice can do to address their specific dental health or cosmetic concerns, or what treatment (that you can provide) is right for them. Alongside those results, they get free, high-value content from you that helps them analyze their results. On the flip side, as they head into your coliseum, you get an incredible amount of data on them that informs where you want to seat them. For example, on Dr. Klauer's website, tmjsleepindiana.com, site visitors are prompted to "Take the Sleep Quiz" when they've scrolled halfway through the home page.

THE MAGIC OF GOOD QUIZ/ASSESSMENT MARKETING IS THAT IT IS THE PUREST POSSIBLE VALUE EXCHANGE; BOTH PARTIES GET VALUE.

This kind of lead magnet can be incredibly powerful—both to inform and educate your audience and grow your email list (Attention Audience) but there are a few key lessons to be aware of. First, quizzes focused on the individual perform much better than those that assess a team or company. Second, the best quizzes have the clearest, most-simple value proposition. Third, and perhaps most importantly, you must understand that a quiz/assessment is not a survey. A survey is for your benefit—it collects lots of data and gives the survey-taker the same generic response ("thank you for participating in our survey"). A great quiz/assessment provides a highly personalized response that includes not only the quiz-taker's specific results but also context on how to interpret and learn from those results. This is your chance to show off your perspective on this issue and wow the takers with your content.

The other important component of a good quiz within the context of growing your audience is embedding a few "Trojan-horse" questions that help you determine if this is a good lead for your product or service. For example, if you know that much of your yearly revenue comes from Invisalign patients, you might ask quiz-takers to rate their happiness with their smile; this is a less-intrusive way to determine whether or not they might seek care for teeth realignment.

Lead generation doesn't happen overnight and Authority Marketing should be viewed as an accelerator, not a silver bullet, but if you approach your marketing efforts with this framework in mind you will position yourself for a much more effective outcome.

YOUR CONTENT MARKETING ROADMAP

In today's media environment every individual and brand is a media outlet—whether they know it or not. Some are influencing a few hundred people on a Facebook page or Snapchat account, while others who have embraced the media mindset we just spoke of own subscription bases larger than their local newspaper.

The third era of Authority is both the most overwhelming and the most exciting time ever to build a business and make an impact with your messaging.

It's overwhelming because it seems as though a new social-media platform or content format pops up daily, and when you add in keeping up with the algorithms that drive content discoverability on those platforms, it's enough to make you want to just close your laptop before you begin.

We get that—but having a media mindset is infinitely more important than being on the cutting edge of technology. The ways you reach your audience today will likely be different from the formats used in even the near future. What won't be different in the future is how you will keep the attention of your audience—by providing entertaining and informative content that gives them value. For the entirety of the second era, the media owned our attention by leveraging their monopoly on distribution. Now you can use the same mindset to own the third era—but only if you embrace the opportunity!

What holds many experts back from diving in on content marketing is a belief that "the marketing team should handle that." Although a good marketing team is incredibly important to building your Authority, to be seen as an Authority you must personally be a key part of the equation.

ALTHOUGH A GOOD MARKETING TEAM IS INCREDIBLY IMPORTANT TO BUILDING YOUR AUTHORITY, TO BE SEEN AS AN AUTHORITY YOU MUST *PERSONALLY* BE A KEY PART OF THE EQUATION.

The public is moving its attention from large general-media outlets to micromedia outlets that give them exactly what they are looking for. We're shifting from national sports-radio shows that might occasionally touch on our favorite sport or team to podcasts that focus *exclusively* on what we're interested in. We're moving from heavily edited, formal TV shows to LinkedIn native videos shot on iPhones that teach us about currency trading or how to prepare for the new tax plan. We're also increasingly gravitating away from trusting conglomerate media companies to, instead, giving our attention and trust to individuals we perceive as thought leaders, such as Tim Ferriss, Joe Rogan, or Seth Godin. The podcast hosted by Tim Ferriss was the first business/interview podcast to pass 100 million downloads, giving him one of the biggest owned-media coliseums in the world (as of the printing of this book he is well over 400 million downloads). When Ferriss recommends a book or product, it's akin to what Oprah Winfrey did in the past—with one major exception: he owns the connection to his audience.

How about you? How many patients and clients look to your specific expertise for informative and reliable solutions? How full is your coliseum? It's important to include your current marketing strategies in your Authority blueprint so that you can assess where you are and create a plan for success. The good news is that to be successful you don't need nearly as big an audience as Oprah or Tim Ferriss. In fact, we'd recommend that you target a far more specific niche with your content. Success in building your connection with that niche audience begins with visualizing yourself on stage in your coliseum. If you wouldn't deliver the online content you're creating in a high-profile keynote speech, it shouldn't go out as rented, earned, or owned media as part of your content-marketing mix.

Your Personal Newspaper

Creating entertaining, informative content that provides value to your audience attracts and retains attention. Think of your content marketing as your personal newspaper. The most common content-marketing mistakes we see include:

- ❑ **Sporadic delivery:** would you subscribe to a newspaper when you have no idea when it's being delivered?

- ❑ **Ad-heavy:** Many people oversaturate their newspaper/content strategy with promotional posts. This turns off your subscriber base (and often sends them running for the exits in your coliseum).

- ❑ **Op-eds only:** By far the most common mistake we see from experts is filling their newspaper with op-ed content— meaning all of the content is from your own perspective. This kind of content monologue works well if you're already a household name and your coliseum is full of people who know to pay attention to your expertise. However, for those on the way up in terms of building an audience, this kind of me-first approach to content marketing is not only a slow grind in terms of growth, it's also exhausting— because you have to create everything. The best way to approach content marketing from your stage is to invite as many other people onto stage as possible. That way, each person/business you involve in your content is indebted to you for the opportunity—*plus* they have every reason to share that content with their audience, which drives new people into your coliseum.

So, with these pitfalls in mind, how should you approach your content-marketing strategy? Regardless of the category of media (earned, rented, or owned) or format of the content (text, audio, or video), we recommend you break your content into three big-picture categories:

1. **You-driven content:** We sometimes call this category "evergreen" or "op-ed" content, because it primarily includes your intellectual property. This category is not very impactful before you have an audience in place but becomes more and more important as your audience builds and people know to pay attention to your perspective as an Authority. Examples of this kind of content include:

    ▫ **Evergreen content:** Ideal Authority-driven content works backward from what your target audience is searching for online to provide practical insights based on your expertise. This kind of content generally focuses on broad topics or concepts pertinent to your industry and exists to capture those search results and pull in potential patients. Examples of content in this category include angles like "Four Questions to Ask Before Choosing To Get Veneers" or "Three Brushing Techniques You Need to Know." This can also include a teaching or educational series.

    ▫ **Behind-the-scenes/personality-driven content:** Few things build more affinity with your audience than behind-the-scenes access to your life and/or personality. This can include pictures from the road, humorous anecdotes, stories, and other personal content.

    ▫ **Calls to action:** Authority-driven content includes calls to act upon things that benefit you, be it linking your audience to buy your book or to sign up for some event or activity. Part of being an Authority is serving your audience with products and services that solve their problems—but you want to make sure that you don't overdo it in this category, or you'll fall victim to the ad-driven pitfall detailed earlier.

2. **News-driven content:** David Meerman Scott coined the term "newsjacking" in his popular book of that title, and we believe it makes up an incredibly important piece of your content-marketing strategy on your Authority Marketing journey. While Authority-driven content is primarily focused on those who already know you, to continue with the newspaper analogy, news-driven content is your "front-page news" in terms of timeliness; of course, the magic in such content is that it's front of mind for all three of your audiences (those in and out of your coliseum). Examples of this kind of content include:

   - **Calendar-driven content:** Although you can't predict what news will break in the future, you do have the ability to create an editorial calendar for the year based on the predictable calendar-driven news cycle. This is different in each niche, but global examples include new year, new you; tax season; summer; the holidays; and so on.

   - **Newsjacking:** This kind of content connects your message to what's happening in the news cycle, making your expertise extremely timely for your audience. This could be driven by a high-profile story, a new research study, an innovative new technique, or the launch of a new lecture series. A word of caution, though: If the piece of news is touchy or tragic, tread lightly or not at all—not every high-profile incident is worth connecting to your message.

3.   **Relationship-driven content:** Good reporters and the newspapers they work for don't limit their content to their own perspective. Instead, they rely on the expertise of others to curate the best possible content for their audience. When you involve other people in your content, you not only build a relationship with them, you also give them a reason to point their audience into your coliseum. Content marketing at its best is a relationship-building tool, and relationship-driven content includes:

□   **Strategic tagging within social media:** One of the most effective ways to give your audience valuable content and build relationships with journalists and key influencers in your space is to share their content and tag them along the way. We don't want you to do this in the context of a fan (go beyond saying, "great post")—instead, do this in a peer-to-peer way, adding commentary that only an Authority in the shared space could add.

□   **Hosting an interview series on your blog, via a podcast, or video format (or all three):** An interview series puts you in a position to give value to your audience by showcasing content from the top leaders in your field.

While the first two categories of content are important, the biggest game changer in terms of traction, impact and—frankly—*fun* is the third category. When you have a media mindset, you are comfortable enough in your own Authority to curate content from others as a way to build relationships and give value to your audience. While you-driven content and news-driven content will both make an impact over time, relationship-driven content can make an impact immediately.

Let's look at a quick case study of how relationship-driven content can make such an immediate impact—in this case, via Twitter.

A successful speaker and consultant to international corporations like Colgate, Seventh Generation, and DuPont, Carol Sanford was as skeptical about Twitter as any executive we have ever worked with. She was preparing for the release of her first book and, after putting four years of her life into writing it, she wanted to make sure she left no stone unturned when it came to marketing. While Carol knew how important traditional media coverage from players like *Bloomberg Businessweek,* CNBC, and other top outlets would be to her success, relationship-driven content (Twitter, in particular) was not on her radar.

During our initial phone call, about eight months before her book's release, Carol said, "I'm so excited about getting more active online. I'm ready to make content marketing a priority." We loved Carol's energy and told her that her blog would be a big part of the social-media strategy we developed. "But based on your target market," we added, "Facebook won't play a huge role. A smart relationship-driven Twitter strategy will make a much bigger impact with your audience."

This component of our introductory calls with leaders almost always creates the kind of silence that makes us wonder whether the line has been cut.

"Carol … are you still there?"

Carol broke the silence with a familiar line that perhaps you have even uttered in the past: "Twitter? I don't think anyone cares what I ate for lunch."

When we give presentations about the power of relationship-driven content on Twitter to grow one's platform—including things like helping them build relationships with journalists, influencers, other authors, potential patients, and readers—we often look out on a sea of blank stares. We understand their gut reaction. On the surface, Twitter feels superficial, self-centric, and possibly even silly.

Like everything else within social media, context and connections rule the day, and few platforms make building them more efficient than Twitter.

Within a month of the silence on the phone, Carol had worked through Twitter training and developed a strategy focused on using Twitter as a means to build relationships with journalists and key influencers in her topic area. As a new author—and relatively unknown expert (at least in the media space)—Carol needed to mine every opportunity to connect with influential people, and Twitter offered her that chance.

Almost immediately, she connected with Sam Ford (@SamFord), a popular blogger at Fast Company. Sam had written a blog post that Carol loved, and she retweeted his tweet about the post, adding a "love this piece, Sam" comment. Like many journalists, Sam kept a close eye on his Twitter account and thanked Carol for her comment. From there, Carol and Sam started a conversation on Twitter about what it truly means to be a responsible, sustainable business. The connection was made and when Carol's book released six months later, the front cover featured Sam's endorsement. In the years since then, Sam and Carol have remained friends, and he has opened doors for her that led to connections with MIT Media Labs and several consulting engagements, including a large project with Lowe's.

Were it not for Twitter, however—and Carol focusing on relationship-driven content—she and Sam are unlikely to have ever connected. Realistically, dental practitioners who are using social media to their full advantage are few and far between. Establishing and regularly using a social media platform can not only set you apart from your competitors—if you use it right, it can also mean that you interact with individuals who may go on to become long-term professional connections.

Although Twitter is a great environment for quick connections, we often recommend centering your relationship-driven content on an interview series that lives on your blog, giving you a great bridge to new relationships.

Imagine that you're a consultant trying to get appointments with the same ten local CEOs that everybody else is after. If all you're doing is calling them with a pitch, chances are you're getting ignored. Instead, and rather than pushing a pitch at them, pull them to you with a proposal to participate in an interview series on your blog. Think about it: how often do you get sales pitches? All the time—and most are outright ignored. How often do you get an interview request for a blog or podcast? That would catch your attention, wouldn't it? Interview series can also make clients and patients feel like they're part of a dialogue. Drawing potential and existing clients into a conversation about up-and-coming teeth-whitening technology, for example, will only help to establish you as a recognized Authority in your industry.

> **AND RATHER THAN PUSHING A PITCH AT THEM, PULL THEM TO YOU WITH A PROPOSAL TO PARTICIPATE IN AN INTERVIEW SERIES ON YOUR BLOG.**

The magic in starting an interview series on your blog is threefold:

1. Assuming you are only interviewing smart people with good ideas, your audience is going to benefit from the content.

2. You're changing the nature of your interaction with that prospect or potential strategic partner. Instead of a normal sales meeting or sales call where you're in a salesperson vs. prospect dynamic (a huge hill to climb), when you interview someone, it becomes a peer-to-peer interaction, which gives you a much more authoritative position.

3. You're giving your interviewee a reason to share the link to your website once it runs. To go back to the coliseum analogy, you're inviting that person on your stage and they're bringing their audience into your coliseum with them.

Content marketing, when used the right way, is a great bridge to new relationships. But it's a rare mindset that sees that and utilizes it; if you can embrace it, you will be playing a game no one else knows is being played.

PR and Media

F

or most experts, PR and media is the crown jewel of the "earned-media" category, and for good reason: few things outside of publishing a book do more for your Authority than media coverage. Almost irrationally we assign buckets and buckets of Authority to someone who has been featured in *Forbes* or interviewed on Fox News, which is why PR and media is such an important part of your Authority blueprint. The magic in such appearances isn't the huge audience you reach—although that's nice, assuming the interview goes well. Rather, it's the ability to remarket that interview and the associated media logo from that point forward to build your Authority.

Being interviewed and featured in the news—radio, television, print, and online—is one of the fastest ways to build credibility and expertise. Being interviewed regularly creates a sense of "omnipresence" while positively building your brand. Additionally, when consumers see "As Seen On/In" with numerous logos of prestigious media outlets, it immediately builds confidence and trust in the mind of the prospect. As mentioned in the branding section of this book, if you aren't yet the brand, the quickest way to build Authority is by association—and few brands are more well-known to your audience than *media* brands.

In a similar way to what we explored with content marketing, the best approach to get PR today is to have a push/pull approach, where you pitch ideas directly to the media. You pitch an article idea on a certain topic, or you pitch yourself as a guest to opine on specific topics. This approach still works, particularly if you're working with a good publicist who has fostered good media relationships.

However, the journalism industry is shifting, and that new landscape is affecting how publicists and marketers approach media. In today's media landscape there are fewer and fewer journalists at traditional media outlets, and those who remain are now tasked with more work than ever. They must fill up the newspaper, the website, and social-media channels with good content. As such, you have more and more marketers pitching fewer and fewer journalists. We talk with media members who get upwards of a thousand pitches a day! That means your pitch is a drop in the bucket. To be frank, unless you have an established brand or existing relationships, it is going to be very hard for you to stand out.

This is another reason why news-driven content is such a vital tool. It allows you to widen your net around certain topics, as statistics show that journalists are increasingly turning to Google, Twitter, Help A Reporter Out, News & Experts, and other online resources when they need an expert to speak on a breaking news topic. When you have created a "newsjacking" post, you widen your net to attract media to you rather than trying to stand out among a thousand daily pitches. This also facilitates relationship-building with media personalities. Media members are more frequently looking to build these kinds of relationships with Authorities, and if you are doing the same—à la Carol Sanford and her Twitter connection with influencer Sam Ford, you give yourself a much better chance to build these kinds of connections.

Another thing we want to consider when it comes to PR and media is the value of publicity. There are essentially three different levels of value on the publicity front:

1.   The first level is the audience you reach. If you're doing a live TV or radio interview, or you've gotten an article published, the most obvious and direct piece of value is the audience that will see, listen to, or read the piece of publicity. They hear you speak or read your article and decide to hire you for a speech or buy a book from you. That's what most people are concerned with when it comes to PR and media; they want to sell something or promote their services or products to that audience.

2.   The second level of value, which is actually much more important in terms of building lasting Authority, is the ability to *remarket* that media coverage. When you have an article in *Forbes*, for example, that *Forbes* logo can go on

your website and in your marketing materials for the rest of your career. That mention of *Forbes* becomes part of the way you're introduced on TV or at speaking engagements. The remarketing of media coverage and the Authority by association that comes with being featured on major media outlets is one of the most important pieces of value that comes from publicity. If you're reading this book and you have not done media, then you don't have media brand logos to showcase, and you should know that is one of the most important levers you can pull to quickly ramp up your Authority.

WHEN YOU HAVE AN ARTICLE IN *FORBES*, FOR EXAMPLE, THAT *FORBES* LOGO CAN GO ON YOUR WEBSITE AND IN YOUR MARKETING MATERIALS FOR THE REST OF YOUR CAREER.

---

3.   The third level of value in publicity is also very important. It goes back to an idea we have talked about a few times in this book: the idea of not just entertaining and engaging audiences, but actually siphoning off that audience by giving people a reason to head to your coliseum via the lead magnet you offer. In other words, you're using that interview or article to drive people back to your owned media and grow your email list. That's why it is so important to have the right lead magnet in place, so you

really maximize your value from any publicity. Without that, you will only be benefitting from a fraction of the value you could be getting from publicity opportunities.

A final point on PR and media is that in today's world it has become easy to track your audience. In the past, people would have to ask, "What's the ROI? How do I know for sure that your interview led to me getting patients?" That's always been a tough question for PR firms to handle. But now, thanks to data-mining and analytics, we have the ability to track which people are interacting with which content online. Who actually likes your article? Who shared it? Who's tweeting about it? How many people came to your website from the article?

When it comes to PR and media, it's important to have a strategy in place to maximize the value that any publicity may bring. It's also imperative to track that internet activity to understand where that value is coming from. This is yet another way in which the new media landscape is creating opportunities for anyone interested in marketing his or her Authority.

Speaking

f PR and media are perceived as the crown jewel of Authority in the minds of most experts, as they're what people most associate with growing their Authority, keynote speaking isn't far behind. Speaking can create significant income streams through fees alone, but the opportunity to sell product in the back of the room, generate leads and interest from the audience, and co-opt other people's patients to become your patients makes speaking one of the most desired and sought-after of all Authority Marketing pillars, and therefore an integral part of your blueprint.

There are a lot of successful businesspeople who want to do more speaking and are puzzled as to why they're not getting more opportunities. The main reason would be that they're not well positioned online as a speaker. They're on as a business owner or a financial planner—an operator or commodity instead of an Authority. If your brand is not built to offer a speaker online, at least partially, you will have trouble landing the speaking engagements you want. The reason being that you will be seen more as a vendor or potential sponsor than a speaker.

It all comes back to branding. As you'll recall from the branding section of this book, there are two phases to creating an image in the minds of your audience, the first of which is pre-interaction. If you are under consideration for a speaking engagement and the meeting planner Googles your name and lands on a corporate website where you're featured as one of many on the "leadership team," that meeting planner is likely going to forward your submission to her sponsorship chair to hit you up for a booth in the exhibit hall! Whereas if he or she Googles your name and lands on your personal brand website and the first image is you on stage giving a keynote speech, he or she is much more likely to envision you as a main stage educator rather than a lunchtime breakout sponsorship speaker.

This is a key reason why we encourage people to plant a flag for themselves as an Authority with a stand-alone website, as that is a place where you can be featured as a mission-driven thought leader, speaker, and media personality. It connotes a whole different brand than a corporate website that lists you as practice owner. Again, if we are planning an event and you pitch me your corporate website, we are going to encourage our sponsorship chair to get you to pay $15,000 for a booth at our conference. But if we get a link to a speaking page on a stand-alone website where you're a published author and we see a photo of you giving a keynote speech, perhaps even find a video of you giving speeches, our perception shifts. Now, we are wondering how much of our budget we need to set aside to get you to our event as we sweat whether or not you're going to ask for first-class accommodations in addition to your speaking fee.

The second phase of branding yourself as a speaker involves the assets you have in place. It's best to have three key assets. First, you want a speaker's kit within your website. This is a two- to four-page PDF attachment that can be downloaded or sent to those requesting more information about you as a speaker. This includes your bio, three to five popular keynote topics you can speak to, logos from past events and media appearances, and ideally quotes from people who have heard you speak.

Secondly, you need a promotional speaker's reel—a highlight video that really establishes you as an elite keynote speaker. Such a video is typically two to four minutes long and provides highlights from several different speeches. You can include media logos and associations, as well.

The third key asset you want to have is a raw ten- to twenty-minute unedited video of you on stage giving a keynote speech. This is being requested more and more frequently by event planners. This is really what the meeting planner, the person who's actually on the hook for whether or not you deliver on stage, is looking for. What tends to really sell them is the unedited twenty-minute video. He or she may sell you to their board or the powers that be with your speaker kit and highlight reel—but only if convinced to do so by your raw video.

If you want to get speaking engagements, it's imperative to have those three assets.

So, now that you know how to market yourself as a speaker, common questions that follow are, "Where do I speak?" and "Do I speak for free or charge a fee?" Let's start with the second question.

Most people start speaking for free. This allows them to gain experience and develop those visual assets we just discussed. It affords an opportunity to get video and pictures of them speaking. It also brings other speaking opportunities. In the beginning, most speaking opportunities come from people who were sitting in the audience of a previous speech. In other words, giving a speech for free excites people and translates into additional speaking engagements.

The more a person speaks, the higher his or her Authority rises, thus affording the ability to call more shots about where he or she speaks and what the context is. Once a speaker has established Authority, he or she can start charging a speaking fee. However, there will be certain conferences where the audience is of such high quality—where it is such a value to be on stage—that it may be best to waive a speaking fee. This is especially true if the audience is composed of potential patients.

Imagine yourself in such a position. If you know you can generate $50,000 out of that audience through a few of them becoming patients at your practice, then it may be worth speaking for free rather than a fee. But first you must get to a point in your career where those decisions are your own and not someone else's.

Now, back to the question of *where* you should speak. Speaking engagements are either in person or virtual. In-person events within your local market are easy to do. If they're outside your local market, that requires a commitment, which likely involves the friendly skies. The events which are going to provide the biggest value to you are those most concentrated in your highest-value lead bases. These may not be the most popular or glamorous conferences; they might not have the largest social-media shares, but if the right twenty to fifty people are in the room, that makes all the difference. If you get a small group from the niche audiences you want to target, that can be much more powerful and beneficial to you than speaking to a thousand people who are not your potential patients. Remember, *the riches are in the niches.*

With in-person events, it's important to consider the amount of time it is going to take you. Then weigh that against the likelihood that you're going to get a significant return on your investment of time and resources. If you do decide to attend a large in-person event, there is one thing you absolutely must be sure to do—get professional photos! If you speak at a big event—especially where there is a great backdrop—and you don't get professional photos, you are missing a massive opportunity. Don't just have your family snap some shots with their phones; spend $500 and hire a professional photographer. These types of photos can be immensely valuable for your website and speaking packages.

Another key thing to remember is that most speaking engagements live in the earned-media category. As such, we encourage you to keep the same one-two punch mindset in place that we've encouraged throughout this book. The first area of focus is delivering great content—obviously you need to crush it on stage—but the second area of focus is siphoning off as much of this audience as possible and driving them back to your coliseum.

There are two ways to leverage a lead magnet (such as quiz/assessment) in conjunction with a speaking engagement. The first and most obvious is using it as a call to action at the end of the speech: "For everyone in the audience who is curious about what they can do in their community to spread dental health education to elementary and middle schools, head to ShareDentalKnowledge.com and sign up to receive my personal newsletter." The second and perhaps even better way to do it is to send the meeting planner who booked you a link to your assessment a month in advance of the speech and ask him or her to share it with all attendees, so you can share the audience data as you give your presentation. This positions you as a data-driven, hyper-personalized speaker, this is exactly what most meeting planners are looking for—and it gives you a way to get the audience's contact information ahead of the speech. Most meeting planners won't be willing to give you an email list of the audience, but—if you package your request in a way that gives huge value to your presentation—they will indirectly give you access to that list. In addition to delivering a more personalized speech thanks to the data from the audience, you have also just added a lot of people to the seats of your Attention Audience in your coliseum.

THE OUTCOMES OF AUTHORITY

Lead Generation

Which is more important to the success of a business: lead generation or sales?

Although there are loud voices on both sides of this debate, the practical answer for most businesses is simply "yes" because most have to climb both hills to grow practices.

The first hill of growth is generating leads for a practice. This is difficult to do in any business climate but particularly so in today's environment of noise and disruption.

For the few practices who are lucky enough to climb this first hill successfully, they must now summit a second, bigger hill by convincing as many of those leads as possible to choose their practice. The problem in this equation is the word "convince," as most believe they have to resort to tactics like discounting or commoditizing their product or service to motivate action but in reality either push prospects away or cannibalize their own margins in the process.

THE HIGH GROUND OF AUTHORITY

The reason Authority is so valuable for entrepreneurs and leaders is that instead of having to drag uninterested leads up the second hill of sales (like most practice owners), you begin on what Dan Kennedy calls "the high ground of Authority" and qualified leads are so drawn to you that they summit the hill on their own in a quest to learn—and then buy. You put yourself in such a position of leverage that not only can you filter which leads you allow to buy but also at what price and under what terms.

This is counterintuitive for most entrepreneurs and leaders because it argues against something many of us were taught, which is that sales is the most important skill an entrepreneur can have.

But that's not true—people don't want to be sold something, they want to buy something that solves a problem for them—and the best way to get someone to buy something from you is to position yourself as the unquestionable Authority in your space, someone they would be lucky to have a chance to work with. As such, they are willing to climb a hill and then ask permission to do so. If patients are going to invest their time, well-being, and money into your practice, they will be most likely to do so once they are convinced—through several different avenues, ideally—that you are the best person for the job.

But don't let your perch of Authority positioning cause you to lose sight of the first hill of growth that you must climb very intentionally with your audience—lead generation.

LEAD GENERATION

We get it—you've been waiting for the "lead-generation" portion of this book, which perhaps was the reason you initially picked it up. Many who utilize Authority Marketing do so with the intention of growing a practice and/or personal brand. To grow, you must help more patients and/or do more business with the patients you already have. Leveraging Authority position in your industry, community, or marketplace to generate a higher volume of qualified leads—a magnet with leads flowing toward you—is one of the most effective ways to monetize Authority Marketing. Part of your Authority blueprint includes assessing how you currently generate leads and how that process might be improved.

The big question we encourage you to ask as you look at your current lead generation process is this: "Am I approaching lead generation with a marketing mindset or with a media mindset?" As a reminder, a marketing mindset is a dated way to look at lead generation that looks at one conversion—*how many people did I create impressions with and how many of those people immediately raised their hand to learn more or schedule an appointment?* This is an expensive and ineffective way to approach lead generation because most people aren't ready to make an appointment or consultation the first time they learn about you. As such, if this is how you are approaching lead generation it's likely you're spending a significant amount of money for very little results.

Instead, we want to encourage you to have a media mindset, which looks at an additional conversion beyond the "fast-track" leads: *how many people did I create impressions with and how many of those people extended their interaction with me based on joining my list?* This kind of mindset provides you with one of the most important outcomes of Authority Marketing: leverage, which you get in spades as you grow your attention audience. This audience provides not only predictable lead flow (for example: on average, out of every 100 people that take the assessment, 11.4 will raise their hands within 6 months for a meeting) but also a group of people that can amplify your message.

We will talk more about the concept of lead velocity in the next section but if you don't approach lead generation with a media mindset, you're setting yourself up for a very expensive, ineffective approach to generating leads.

Patient Conversion

Converting leads into patients is what makes the world of dentistry go round, but those who succeed understand that, in today's landscape, conversion is much more about positioning than prospecting.

Think about it—when is the last time you bought something as a result of cold outreach or sales-driven prospecting?

It's been a while, right?

Whereas sales used to do the heavy lifting in past business climates, today marketing does the hard work by cutting through the noise to position you the right way so that patients are coming to you as opposed to running for the hills because they're being sold.

AUTHORITY POSITIONING

We talked at length in this book about the importance of positioning in both phase one and two and why the way your audience views you is the single biggest influence on whether or not they purchase, refer, and stay as your patient.

Although there are many things that drive positioning, the most important drivers of Authority positioning include your book, authority-by-association, content marketing, speaking, and PR.

But it's not enough to just have those items on your website or on the walls in your office. Instead, make sure you drive consistent conversion of the leads you generate by packaging those items up and educating your prospects over and over again.

The mistake most people make is that they assume far too much about the awareness of their prospects.

Never make assumptions. Don't just say you were featured in *Forbes*, interviewed on CNBC, or spoke at TEDx—they may not find that. Send it to them! Then send it again in another form.

One of the best ways to start the conversion process is to use a "shock & awe" package to overwhelm your prospect with value while reinforcing your Authority positioning.

For example, if someone in your Attention Audience (your email list) raises their hand for a free consultation with you, you want to do more than high five your marketing team and set up the appointment. Instead, FedEx a shock & awe package to that prospect that includes your book and other materials that both (A) give value and (B) reinforce your positioning. Remember how Dr. Klauer sends his incoming new patients chapters of his book—and when time permits, a physical copy in the mail—before they even arrive in office? Aim for that kind of "wow" factor.

But don't stop there. After your conversation extend your interaction with them toward a very clear next step that is accompanied by an additional shock & awe communication.

When you do this and you are competing against others who are going through the normal sales motions, you give yourself an unfair advantage against your competitors.

THE MONEY PYRAMID

Speaking of monetization, once someone is ready to buy, what will you sell them?

To maximize the financial impact of Authority Marketing it's important to first assess your offerings. Ideally, you will have at least three tiers of offerings, creating a money pyramid of products or services, with your most accessible, cheapest offering at the bottom.

Typically, what we see in businesses is that 20 percent of customers deliver 80 percent of profitability. Ideally, you want to grow that 20 percent, and the best way to do that is to make sure you have lower-tier offerings that appeal to the other 80 percent of your patients. You want a stair step of offerings, working up from your most affordable services or products to your most expensive, most exclusive offerings. A lot of businesses make the mistake of only offering that bottom tier, missing the opportunity to offer their elite fans a chance to be part of a high-priced, exclusive group. Some businesses, on the other hand, only focus on the top tier, thus missing the chance to sell to individuals that may have some interest but aren't ready to spend a lot.

Let's use an individual practice's offerings as an example. At the very bottom of the pyramid, there may be a book or a consultation that serves as an entry-level product. The next level up would be their lowest-priced service, perhaps a general teeth-cleaning and examination. It's affordable and accessible for most. It also doesn't take much time for the practice owner, since dental assistants take care of most general cleanings. If this practice owner is a prosthodontist, for example, they might have tiered offerings of crowns and veneers that meet patients' various price points. Their highest tier, full dental reconstruction, offers higher-paying patients exclusive access to the best in reconstructive technology, and unprecedented access to you, the Authority.

As you go up your money pyramid, services become higher priced and more exclusive. Patients generally don't start at the top, they work their way up. The more people you can convert to patients, the more will eventually climb that pyramid. If you aren't offering enough tiers, you won't be converting leads to patients as effectively as you can.

Take an audit of your current offerings. How many levels are there? Put a dollar amount next to each level in that pyramid. Often, this can be an eye-opening exercise. You might realize your pyramid is top heavy and you aren't offering enough lower-end products or services. If so, a book is a great entry-level product. E-learning products are another great way to monetize leads. If your pyramid isn't high enough, consider adding exclusive, high-priced offerings that might appeal to your elite patients.

The great thing about a lead-generation funnel setup like this is that it works while you're sleeping or on vacation or away at a conference. With the right kind of offerings, you will be able to walk into someone else's auditorium and then have a large audience follow you out the door back to your auditorium. It allows you to leverage rented or earned media to maximize the impact of your owned media.

In fact, once you've properly established your Authority and broadened out your lead generation funnel and money pyramid, you will be able to take advantage of inbound marketing rather than having to depend solely on the outbound variety. *Inbound* marketing is when people find you. It's like using a scented bait that attracts fish, as opposed to just throwing a net into the water and hoping to catch whatever happens to swim under the boat. Using the power of a book and the power of Authority to generate leads brings people to you rather than having to go after them.

That's not to say *outbound* marketing doesn't work. It does. You pay money, you get a booth at a trade show, and people are going to come up to you and get interested in what you do. You can direct-mail people or advertise on television or on the radio. It's all outbound and it will get results. But it also requires money and time.

When you become an Authority, *people head to higher ground to find you*. They see that you wrote a book on the topic, or perhaps they read articles you've written online. At that point, they see you as a trusted source and a knowledgeable insider in your field. They'll then contact you because of your Authority. This is a game changer, because the quality of an inbound lead is likely to be much higher than any resulting from outbound marketing.

Retention / Referrals

The Word of Mouth Marketing Association reports that every day in the United States there are approximately 2.4 billion brand-related conversations.

How many of those 2.4 billion conversations revolve around your brand? Are you currently doing anything to ensure that you spark more positive ones in the future? In dentistry, it's no secret that referrals are one of the best and most reliable ways to ensure new patients—ones who will be likely to return again and again.

Few words are better to hear early in a conversation with a new lead than "I was referred by…"

That line changes the dynamic immediately because of the level of trust that is already in place based on their friend vouching for your product or service and allows you to immediately shift from convincing them why you're the best person to solve their problem to actually solving it.

In addition to being the best source of "fast-track" leads, referrals provide a shot of validation to leaders that patients and partners are impressed enough with the product or service to talk about it to others.

However, even though there are many reasons to love referrals, far too many dentists and practice owners get trapped into an overreliance on them to bend their growth curve. In fact, when we ask dentists how they drive leads for their practice many will puff their chests out a bit and say something along the lines of "we're entirely built on referrals."

That kind of response tells us two things about a practice: (1) they have a great operational business that is overdelivering for customers (the foundation of every successful business) and (2) they are likely growing at a slow rate, particularly if they are sitting back and waiting for patients to refer rather than intentionally driving those referrals.

Of course they are puffing their chests out based on #1 but #2 secretly is keeping them up at night because they have no direct control over their lead flow. We discussed this earlier in the book but it bears repeating here—if you rely on referrals for a significant percentage of your lead flow and you aren't doing anything to intentionally drive them, you're beholden to both the willingness and happenstance opportunity your patients have to refer you.

The good news is that a phase-two-reliant practice is usually a sign of a very good operational business. If patient experience wasn't good, those referrals wouldn't be flowing in, right? The bad news is that when you rely entirely on other people to drive lead flow you put yourself in a risky position, because you have limited direct impact on lead generation. Sure, you have plenty of indirect influence on driving referrals by doing a great job for patients, but true referral marketing is a shift from sitting back and passively waiting for referrals to actively driving them.

Put simply—you are sitting around waiting for the phone to ring.

This is a helpless feeling for a practice owner, but it is the reality for many—even when they do great work!

We'll leave doing the great work to you but in this book let's explore the art of referral marketing and why it is such an important component of your Authority Marketing Blueprint.

WHY DO PEOPLE REFER?

There are thousands of country clubs in the United States and many of them battle the exact same challenge: driving more memberships.

Millions of dollars are spent each year on branding, advertising, direct mail, social media, open houses, young family programs, camps, and other promotional campaigns meant to drum up interest in joining the club.

However, it's often a very tough sell, as country clubs are competing with public golf courses, neighborhood pools, restaurants, and other pulls on expendable income. The increased competition is one of the reasons this industry is on the decline.

Although many country clubs recognize that referrals from their existing members are the quickest way to achieve new member goals, very few of them understand how to properly motivate those members to actively and excitedly refer their friends.

There are two reasons why we refer others to products or services:

1.   We believe the product or service is something that will delight that person and we're willing to stand behind it.

2.   Our ability to refer others to that product or service is something that makes us look good.

Think about it: typically the referral you are most proud to make is the one where there is an air of scarcity or Authority involved.

- ❑ "The new five-star restaurant downtown is booked out a month, but I know the owner. I'll work on getting you and your in-laws a table."

- ❑ "Sorry to hear about your injury. Have you seen Dr. Mahr yet? He's the best shoulder surgeon in the south and he's typically booked out eight months but let me reach out to him and see if he'll make an exception for you."

- ❑ "My executive coach only takes on eight clients a year and he hasn't had an opening for the past three years but I'll reach out to him and see about getting you on the waiting list."

What's consistent about each of these referrals? The person making the referral is excitedly doing so because it makes them look good by having access to a velvet rope referral. Everyone else is standing in a line around the block, but here, come to the VIP line and let me personally get you to the front of the line.

Sure each of these businesses probably provides a wonderful product or service, but the true motivation for referrals goes far beyond that—it's much more connected to the Authority Halo that such a referral provides for the person making the referral. In the end, good Authority-driven referral marketing creates a win-win-win for you, your patient, and your new lead.

- ❑ You generate leads more consistently and with the expectation of an up-market experience based on the exclusivity.

- ❑ Your patient actively and excitedly refers you as much as they can because of the Authority Halo it delivers to them in the minds of others.

❑ Your new lead gets the benefit of having a chance to consume your product or service and be better off as a result of doing so.

Let's head back to the country club conundrum for a second. The quickest way for a country club to begin a race to the bottom is to run a campaign focused on discounts or new-member specials.

This campaign does two things that work against its goals of adding new members:

1. It makes current members question the value of their membership because of the "on the cheap" approach.

2. It turns a membership into a price-based commodity for potential members, which dilutes the attraction.

A much better approach would have been to announce—with the largest possible exposure—that the club is no longer taking on new members. This kind of announcement creates excitement, intrigue, and interest among existing members and the community because a velvet rope has now been placed around the property.

All of a sudden the country club is viewed differently from those both inside and outside the ropes. Members who weeks earlier were complaining about the lukewarm water cooler on #13 or the coloration on the #7 green are walking a bit taller and looking for as many opportunities as possible to wear anything with that country club logo on it. Conversations at weddings and other events hosted there feature comments like this: "Did you know this place isn't taking on new members anymore? I'm kicking myself—I had a chance to join a few years back and should have…"

All of a sudden that country club has a brand that is long on Authority, which shifts the dynamic for all involved. Instead of having to ask members to refer friends or creating dynamic referral campaigns, members now beg to get their friends to the top of the waiting list.

Put simply: nothing makes us want to refer like the ability to unhook a velvet rope and walk our friends to the front of the line. It's counterintuitive, but the best way to drive referrals to your business is to channel your inner Augusta National (and Dan Kennedy) and go heavy on both Authority and exclusivity.

DOES YOUR BRAND ENCOURAGE OTHERS TO REFER?

Few industries are harder to break intro and thrive in as speaking. And there are numerous dynamics that drive the growth of a few speakers and the bottom-of-the-barrel scraping that most speakers end up doing.

Many speakers are frustrated because they believe they are the absolute best in class in their given topic area yet others who "don't have near the quality I do" seem to consistently take the stage while they sit in the crowd.

It's important to understand that being best in class is just the starting point to driving referrals.

One of the key things Authority provides you is a brand that people want to refer to because it makes them look good for having access to you. As a speaker, if your website, speaker's reel, speaker's kit, and other social media assets don't accelerate trust and position you as the top Authority in your space, even those who know and love you are going to be nervous about referring.

DO YOU HAVE CLARITY ON WHO IS REFERRING YOU?

Many leaders make the mistake of focusing their referral marketing efforts only on customers, which limits the reach of such campaigns.

The reality is that most practices have three key categories of referral drivers:

- ❑ Patients

- ❑ Referral partners/strategic partners (typically other practices and offices)

- ❑ Influencers (typically individuals who benefit from referring you)

If you don't currently have a way to track the sources of your referrals, you must put such a system in place. Depending on volume, you may be able to start with something as simple as an Excel document with three tabs (one for each of the categories above). Use these tabs to organize both existing referral bases and ones you want to target.

Once you have a clear view of who is referring you right now, the next step is to think about how you can better empower them to refer you more often in the future. One of the most effective ways to empower each of the groups above is to involve them in your content-marketing efforts.

As we discussed earlier in this section, the best way to give people a reason to share your content is to feature or involve them in it. One way to do this is through an interview series, which you can use to both empower existing relationships and build new ones with people you don't yet know. Additionally, you can feature referral partners, patients, and others in evergreen or news-driven content in a positive way, which will encourage them to push it out to their audience. Another way to empower your audience is to create high-quality content that they organically want to share with their friends, family, and contacts via social media. None of us want to share content that is promotional or marketing driven; we want to share content that is smart, vulnerable, funny, or educational, and the more you develop such content, the more people want to share it.

You also have to find ways to make people want to refer you more. Don't worry, we're not going to ask you to call them and ask, "What can I do to make referring me easier?" or "Do you have anyone you can refer me to?" In fact, we're going to caution you against ever doing something like that, because it removes any ounce of scarcity and Authority from the referral relationship. You want these groups to feel lucky that you're allowing them to refer people to you at all— that you're giving them unique access no one else is getting, like the country club. The more omnipresence your brand has, the more this impression will be organically communicated. Another great way to intentionally create this environment is to consistently garner earned media attention that elevates your reputation and prestige.

YOU WANT THESE GROUPS TO FEEL LUCKY THAT YOU'RE ALLOWING THEM TO REFER PEOPLE TO YOU AT ALL—THAT YOU'RE GIVING THEM UNIQUE ACCESS NO ONE ELSE IS GETTING.

EMPOWERING PATIENTS TO TALK

One of our favorite examples of empowering patients via content marketing comes from a city with a remarkable growth vibe in place: Detroit. Dr. Jamie Reynolds (www.askdrreynolds.com) is a longtime Member of the Advantage Family and, alongside his partner Dr. Larry Spillane, leads one of the fastest-growing orthodontic practices in the Midwest, Spillane & Reynolds (www.myamazingsmile.com).

Rusty was recently in Detroit to speak at an event Dr. Reynolds and Dr. Spillane hosted for dentists in the city and got a chance to tour the newest of their four locations in the growing suburbs of the city. The vibe was fantastic—incredible attention to detail on the branding and plenty of things for kids to do while they are waiting— but what caught our eye was something that seemed out of place in a normal orthodontic practice: a giant gong.

It's no surprise that lead-flow at most dental and orthodontic practices relies heavily on referrals from patients, so it's not unusual that Spillane & Reynolds focuses so heavily on patient experience. What is unusual (and awesome) is the way they empower happy patients and their families to drive those referrals.

The referral marketing process at most practices goes something like this: patient finishes last appointment and walks up to the counter with her parents to pay the final bill. During the interaction the front desk clerk is coached to let the patients know that referrals are the lifeblood of the practice and then ask, "Do you know anyone who could benefit from being treated here?" as she pushes a couple of postcards toward the patient.

That is *super* awkward for everyone involved.

Instead of going with that transactional (and ineffective) approach to referrals, Dr. Reynolds and Dr. Spillane instead focus on empowering patients and their families to talk about the "wow" experience they provide, including very intentionally creating a "referral moment" along the way, which brings us back to the gong.

When a patient gets their braces off, everyone in the office stops what they're doing—from the front desk all the way to back office staff—and gathers around the gong in the main practice room. Other patients turn and watch as well as the teen, with a fresh new smile, bangs the gong as everyone cheers in the background. Not only is that an authentic, super-memorable moment for that teen, but unlike the mom who was attempted to be coerced into referring with the postcard gimmick, the mom of the teen that is hitting the gong can't get that video on Instagram and Facebook quickly enough. Of course when she posts it she's not only talking about Samantha's great new smile, she's talking about how awesome Spillane & Reynolds have been along the way.

This kind of "referral moment" creates a true win-win because the content is something that the referring party actually is excited to share and it empowers them to talk about one of the best "phase two" orthodontic experiences in the entire country at Spillane & Reynolds.

Are you creating win-win moments with your patients, strategic partners, and connected influencers that empower them to talk about you and your business in ways they are excited to take part in?

Here are some examples of win-win moments that empower referral marketing:

❑ The interview series we discussed earlier is one of the most effective ways to empower others to talk about your practice. When you interview someone on your podcast you give them a reason to push their audience over to you to listen to it. When they share such an interview they are typically going to wax on about their experience with you because it's easier and more comfortable to do than for them to share it and say what an awesome interview they gave.

❑ One of the reasons publishing a book is such a powerful referral marketing tool is not only your name on the front of it but, perhaps as importantly to the growth of your business, all of the other names that you feature throughout it. Consider what strategic partners, influencers, and target relationships you can feature in your book to not only build goodwill but also empower those people to help you promote the book, which of course they're going to be more excited to do because they're in it.

❑ Red-carpet-style backdrops at events that feature logos in a creative and well-designed way give people a great reason to share photos from your event.

❑ Murals or backdrops on walls in brick and mortar locations do exactly the same thing when they are well-designed. In most cities around the country you'll find Instagram-worthy backdrops that empower tourists and locals to talk about the city. If you can create something similar in your actual office, you'll do the same.

❑ Events are one of our favorite ways to empower referral marketing. Let's say you have a new book coming out—that presents a tremendous opportunity for a high-value event. Rather than hosting a "lunch and learn" or other commoditized educational event, host a book-launch party or an "evening with the author" at a high-value venue and tell your patients and referral partners they are welcome to invite a certain number of friends. This creates both scarcity and prestige for those patients or partners who are now motivated to bring friends, because it's an event their friends are likely to see significant value and Authority in (which makes them look good).

Referral marketing should be integrated across each of the pillars of Authority Marketing as an accelerant of the process. We spent a lot of time in this letter talking about how to leverage branding and content marketing to drive referrals, but each of the pillars can do so, from events to speaking.

NOW THAT YOU HAVE YOUR BLUEPRINT—WHAT'S NEXT?

Now you not only understand what Authority Marketing is and how it can be a game changer for your practice, you also have an understanding of what an Authority Marketing blueprint looks like and how to go about building your own.

In this section of the book, we've broken down Authority Marketing and given you an insider's look at each piece of it, from the foundation to the outcomes. You now know the difference between earned, rented, and owned media, as well as earned, rented, and owned events, and you've seen how to integrate each to maximize value in the new media landscape. You have the information you need to market yourself as a speaker, plus you understand the value of newsjacking and how to employ push/pull strategies when it comes to media.

In Part III of our book, we will teach how to start implementing your Authority Marketing blueprint. We'll talk you through the process of writing a book; using earned, rented, or owned media to market your Authority; and how to maximize lead generation.

PART III

IMPLEMENTING YOUR AUTHORITY MARKETING BLUEPRINT

BEGINNING WITH THE END IN MIND

Whenever we talk with dentists about the impact of Authority Marketing, we like to ask how they will measure success. Most people intuitively understand how Authority can benefit them, but many don't have an exact idea of how they're going to measure their success along the way. Very often, success and failure are more subjective and instinctive than they are objective or data-driven. It's important to resist the magnetism of the subjective route and instead create hard metrics that can be put up on a board to gauge the success of your Authority Marketing efforts.

For some individuals, metrics do not matter. People have different motivations and goals for pursuing an Authority Marketing journey. For some, it could be making an impact or advancing a cause. In instances like these, success isn't always based on a black and white metric. That's fine, but you need to be clear about that up front. For most people, however, Authority Marketing is a route to growing a practice and freeing up more time to spend with your family or pursue personal interests. To gauge that kind of success, you need to have concrete metrics and know exactly what you're aiming for.

Beginning with the end in mind is rule number two from Stephen Covey's iconic book, *The 7 Habits of Highly Successful People*. It's undeniably true; the most successful people start with a vision of what they want the end to look like. We believe this should be emphasized whenever any professional is undertaking an Authority Marketing initiative. You have to know what success looks like and where you want to end up. If you don't, how will you know if you're happy with the results?

Once you have your end in mind, the specific strategy will be informed in such a way as to help you reach that desired end. This roadmap should have checkpoints along the way to make sure you're tracking toward your desired end goal. We have seen many an Authority Marketing journey veer off course, and only those who set unemotional, data-driven benchmarks have the clarity to swerve back on the road.

For example, perhaps one of your goals is to use your enhanced Authority status to generate three hundred new patients in the first year. As we have discussed throughout this book, it can take time to build a large audience and fill your coliseum, but along the way you can leverage your content marketing to work toward that specific objective. For example, you can use relationship-driven content on your blog as an engine to build relationships with potential clients. Writing a blog (and most certainly a book) becomes a tool to expand your network. Featuring key individuals or companies on your blog (and in your book) presents huge opportunities. Those companies and individuals will more readily promote both if they're featured by you.

But if you don't have clarity on what you're looking to get out of the Authority-building process, then you will likely end up spending a lot of time on efforts that may end up off-target, and those can have huge financial consequences. On the flip side, if you work backward from your end goal, you may be like many authorities who see immediate and substantial returns on their time and investment because of the business development impact they are able to make.

Knowing what success looks like for you and what metrics you will use to gauge it means you can work toward them from the very start. Although big-picture goals can be similar, the vision is different for everyone, and there is no right or wrong answer. We always say that Authority is all based on what industry, business, marketplace, and community you are in. Those factors and the goals you have for your business and industry are going to determine what pillars of the Authority Marketing framework you should be concentrating on.

WHO'S RIGHT FOR AUTHORITY MARKETING?

While there are many reasons why an Authority Marketing initiative makes sense, you should only undertake it for pragmatic business or missional purposes. This should not be an exercise in ego. It's not that we have an objection to people satisfying their egos, but you will never be able to spend enough money to become an Authority in the minds of the masses. As we have discussed, trying to become an Authority to people who aren't practitioners themselves, potential patients, or who don't have the capacity to help you make an impact is a foolish endeavor, anyway. Not only is it really expensive to reach the masses, if your topic is broad enough to appeal to the masses, then it likely isn't driving your core business.

WHILE THERE ARE MANY REASONS WHY AN AUTHORITY MARKETING INITIATIVE MAKES SENSE, YOU SHOULD ONLY UNDERTAKE IT FOR PRAGMATIC BUSINESS OR MISSIONAL PURPOSES.

The concept of creating Authority has to be strategically and systematically planned. It has to be built around creating success for you and your business. This is not an exercise in vanity; it's about strategically elevating your Authority to grow your business. Some people get that while others miss the point. The people who become the most effective authorities are those who approach the process with the heart of a teacher—a phrase made famous by an Authority who does just that with incredible skill and generosity: Dave Ramsey.

When it comes to personal finance, Dave Ramsey is the Authority. He is an author, television personality, motivational speaker, and host of the third-largest syndicated radio show in the country. *The Dave Ramsey Show* is heard on more than five hundred radio stations throughout the United States and Canada. It's also available on iOS, iHeartRadio, YouTube, and his website, DaveRamsey.com. At this point in the book, you're probably seeing some patterns. One of those is a benefit of Authority: omnipresence. Ramsey's show is everywhere, but his content can be found across numerous formats, including his numerous *New York Times* bestsellers.

Ramsey embodies the monumental shift we're encouraging you to make in this book—moving from a marketing mindset to a media mindset. Ramsey frequently describes those he recommends as "having the heart of a teacher"—and it is also so true of him. He utilizes his own experience with bankruptcy in a self-deprecating and honest way to do everything he can to prevent others from sharing the fate he himself underwent prior to turning things around.

He is also a very good example of an Authority whose professional visibility doesn't necessarily mean that he is personally doing everything in the business. This is one of the biggest concerns we hear from experts: "I want to be able to delegate more to others in my business and I'm worried that the more visible I become, the more people will want to do business with only me." Managed properly, that's the opposite of what Authority will do for you in your business. Instead, you'll find yourself becoming a force-multiplier for your team—positioning them for greater success, with you as the visionary and mission-driven Authority behind them. The goal of effective Authority Marketing is to take the work you're putting in to deliver content or care to individual leads or clients and amplify it at scale.

Think about what Dave Ramsey has done. He takes the content most financial advisors have to say again and again to individual clients or leads and delivers it at scale in a way only he can; his team can then manage the operations around serving those clients. He now has more than four hundred employees and a multimillion-dollar business built on a foundation of Authority. What we love best about his Authority is that it came about as a result of his media mindset—value first and everything else falls in place.

This is not to say that the people who become successful authorities don't want more than just success. Of course, they want to grow their businesses and make more money. That's a large part of why they're in the process to begin with. But they understand that you grow your business and Authority by serving people. Their mindsets are geared toward providing value to people. When you give people value, they turn around and give value back. That's how markets work.

It goes along with the rule of reciprocity. When you teach people and educate without it being a sales pitch, where there is nothing expected in return, that's when people are more motivated to want to work with you. This is why Authority Marketing is hands down the most rewarding way to build a practice, a reputation, and a legacy.

VISUALIZE YOUR SUCCESS

Since success looks different for everyone, we believe it is helpful to visualize a few of the outcomes that we've seen others achieve as a result of building their Authority. To articulate this, here is a breakdown of the fourteen most common definitions of success we've observed from dealings with would-be authors and authorities.

1.   **Being seen as an Authority, celebrity, or expert.** This means that your name is known within your industry, marketplace, or community, and that people trust you. You are viewed as a go-to individual for the services or products you provide.

     When people think of your industry, they automatically think of you. When the local or national media wants an expert on matters relating to your field, you are the one they call.

     It doesn't matter if you're a real estate agent, dentist, or CEO—this kind of Authority status translates into big gains for your business. And for some, just the status itself is something they relish and view as a worthy end to their Authority Marketing efforts.

2. **Achieving omnipresence and multiplicity.** Your marketing reaches every medium, your name is associated with your industry, marketplace, or community, and you have referral and opportunities coming from a myriad of marketing approaches.

   When someone searches your name on Google, they will need to pack a lunch because there is so much content. You have secured earned media, rented media, and owned media, driving people to your personal coliseum.

   Omnipresence means complete media mastery. Among other things, you are utilizing social media, podcasts, and newsjacking while leveraging your book. Everything is coordinated and strategically aimed at pointing people to your practice.

3. **Recruiting people into your organization.** Your Authority status is acting as a recruiting magnet, pulling exceptionally talented people to you rather than you having to spend time and money looking for them.

   Think about it. If you're Facebook or Google, do you have to spend a lot of time searching for talent? No, when you have that much Authority, people will come to you. They will want to be connected to your Authority.

   When you are an Authority, you can be pickier about who you choose to hire. You can attract the best of the best, rather than spending money to advertise and settling for whoever responds.

4. **Establishing a legacy or making an impact.** You want future members of your company, family, industry, or community to remember you and your vision after you are gone. You want to be remembered for what you have contributed to those around you and for how you saw the world.

Or you want to share insight or knowledge that impacts people's lives or the industry you work in. Perhaps your knowledge can inform the industry going forward or fundamentally change something about it.

Making an impact can be just as subjective as defining success. However, as an Authority you can effect change. It's just a question of what you want to impact.

5. **Changing patients' lives.** Many authorities in dentistry are imparting knowledge that changes the way people look at their health and lifestyle. Or, they're trying to reach more people with their effective practices.

It can be as simple as educating people on how to live healthier lives, starting with teeth and gum health. Or it could be targeting a niche client base—individuals with TMJ or sleep apnea, for example—and educating them on how to overcome the challenges their condition imparts.

You could have an amazing care facility or a breakthrough approach you want more people to be aware of and take advantage of. Regardless of the how, if the goal is changing patients' lives, becoming an Authority can help you achieve those ends.

6. **Educating and spreading knowledge.** You believe your knowledge will educate people and enrich their lives in some way. For you, people having more knowledge is a major goal.

    Perhaps you want to post videos on YouTube or Instagram teaching patients often-overlooked flossing techniques, or educate them about the importance of instilling good dental care habits in children. By writing a book and/or using media to your advantage, you will establish yourself as an Authority and be able to spread your knowledge much further.

7. **Advocating for a cause.** Perhaps there is a nonprofit organization you work with, support, or run. Or there could be a cause that's close to your heart—breast cancer, for example. For you, success means bringing more attention to the issue and generating capital to further that cause.

    We all have causes near to us. But for some, that becomes a personal drive. These people are on a mission to help others. Whatever your cause may be, establishing your Authority and using it to advocate for that cause is a worthy goal.

8. **Generating new patients.** This means that Authority status has created a significant rise in referrals and potential leads.

    For many practices, it all starts with good leads. Without those initial leads, new patients don't come in and the business doesn't function. Authority not only increases the volume of leads; it will increase the quality of your leads. Like we said before, your Authority becomes a lead-generation magnet, as companies and individuals who know of you will be eager to work with you.

9. **Getting PR and media visibility.** You are experiencing a lot of media coverage, perhaps even making media appearances yourself as an expert. This type of visibility comes with a lot of value for businesses and practices.

    Being seen as an expert who appears in the media provides an additional layer of Authority to you and your business. Earlier in the book, we talked about the importance of trust and how Authority can increase the speed of trust. In that light, media appearances and coverage are really amazing tools for gaining trust with potential patients.

10. **Speaking (moving up-market).** You are seeing a higher demand for yourself as a speaker and you have been able to charge higher speaking fees as your Authority climbs. Building your personal brand and Authority allows you to move up-market as a speaker.

    If speaking is a part of your Authority blueprint or something you want to get into, a concrete way to gauge success is the frequency of speaking opportunities and your ability to raise your speaking fee.

11. **Career transitioning.** You have been able to build your Authority and visibility to the point where you can make a career jump and feel confident about landing on your feet.

    Perhaps you want to transition out of the chair and into the business side of your practice, or perhaps you want to venture into a new field, a related field, or even something completely different; Authority allows you to sell yourself as an asset. When you have enough Authority, you become a hot commodity. Even in a new field, you will command respect and trust based on your Authority status.

12. **Selling or buying a business.** If you are in the market to buy a business, having more Authority allows you more power when negotiating. If you are a business or practice no one has heard of, you simply don't have the kind of clout a company like Amazon or Forbes has. That translates to less leverage at the bargaining table.

If you are trying to sell a practice, increased Authority brings in interested parties. Being the go-to for anything, having that kind of established Authority and trust, is going to make your practice an attractive acquisition. Think about it: if you are Amazon looking to buy a grocery store, are you going to buy some chain you've never heard of, or are you going to buy Whole Foods?

13. **Advancing in your career.** You have established yourself as a thought leader or expert within your field and have thus built your practice and your brand in excellence.

Expanding your practice's reach can be tough. Even if you already have the recognition of the population in your surrounding area, you might want to open your coliseum to include regional and even national audiences.

How do you stand out from other dentists and practices in your region? If you've established Authority, you will naturally.

14. **Accomplishing a personal goal.** You always wanted to write a book and take pride in having accomplished that goal.

This may seem like ego, but it is different. For people who just want to write a book, that accomplishment alone is enough. They aren't trying to feed their ego as much as they are trying to accomplish something they see as valuable.

Perhaps it's a bucket-list item, or simply a personal challenge they have given themselves. Whatever it is, the accomplishment of having written a book satisfies their end goal.

These are just some of the definitions of success we see people working toward and achieving through Authority Marketing. It is not by any means definitive, because success looks different for every individual. What's important is understanding what success looks like for *you* from the very beginning. With concrete goals and a strategic Authority blueprint, success can be achieved!

HAPPINESS AND
AUTHORITY MARKETING

s there a connection between Authority Marketing and happiness? Can following an Authority Marketing path actually make you happier?

If you were to ask people what they want out of their lives—or what they want out of their careers, for that matter—the most common answer you would hear is, "I want to be happy." That raises the question, "What is happiness?" What is this elusive concept most people seem to spend their lives chasing?

The truth is that—just like success—happiness means different things to different people. There is no commonly accepted definition of happiness that applies to everybody. It can be pretty hard to create a roadmap to happiness when it's a different destination for each person. In fact, some people couldn't even tell you where that place would be for them.

So, over the course of our careers as entrepreneurs, we have tried to really invest time to determine, "What is happiness and what drives it?" If we know what drives happiness, then we know what things we need to focus our attention and time on.

Over our own careers we've settled on five major drivers of happiness.

The first is **learning and growing.** There's a saying you've probably heard: "You're either growing or you're dying." There is no such thing as staying the same; on this journey, you are either progressing or digressing. The people who are constantly learning and growing are more fulfilled than people who are not. Learning and growing as an individual may mean acquiring new skills, reading new books, teaching yourself a new vocation or occupation, or elevating existing knowledge or skills. People who are focused on professional and personal development tend to be the most content and happiest. This driver of happiness is so powerful that it has become the mission statement of Entrepreneurs Organization (EO), a group that we're both proud to be members of.

The second driver of happiness is having **control over your destiny.** There's nothing more hopeless and discouraging for people than feeling that no matter what effort they put forth, the outcome has already been decided. It feels like you're competing in a rigged system. Why try to be better or do anything different if the results are guaranteed to be the same? When you believe you have no control over your destiny, you essentially lose a positive will to live. So many people get stuck in their careers or in life situations when they feel they have no control over their destiny. How can you really be happy, stuck in such a demoralizing situation?

The third driver is **earned success**, or goal attainment. There is something about earning success that is personally more satisfying and rewarding than just getting something without working for it. Recall a class you took in high school or college where you had to struggle a bit. Maybe you studied every night and joined the study groups; you applied yourself and really invested a lot of time to understanding the material. Then the big test came, and you aced it! That probably gave you a tremendous feeling of success and satisfaction. On the other hand, think of a class where you literally could have slept through it and *still* aced the test. If you don't have to apply yourself at all, getting an A won't give you anywhere near the level of satisfaction you get from the class you actually have to work hard in. In other words, not all A's are equal. When you earn success, you are proud and fulfilled. When you're simply given something, there is no fulfillment. If anything, it creates a sense of entitlement. There is no getting around it: earning success and achieving goals is a huge driver of happiness.

The fourth major driver that we've identified is **quality relationships**. These are not just your professional relationships but important relationships in every facet of your life. Perhaps it's with your parents, your spouse or significant other, your children, your colleagues, or your friends. Whatever relationships mean the most to you, it's important to foster them with time and attention. The more quality relationships people have in their lives, the happier they tend to be. We've seen it time and time again: when you have strained and conflicted relationships, whether it's with parents, your boss, or the couple who lives across the street, it creates friction and frustration. It creates anger and stress—even sadness. All these feelings are the antithesis of happiness.

The final driver of happiness is having an **optimistic future**, which means you are hopeful about what's to come. When you stop having things to look forward to, you might as well hang it up. Perhaps it's looking forward to having an independent life or getting into the career of your dreams. Maybe it means falling in love and getting married. Later, maybe it could be about having children; most parents will say that is one of the greatest joys of life. When the children are grown, there are grandchildren to look forward to. Or *whatever* it is that puts a smile on your face when you look forward to it.

So, in our case anyway, these five things—learning and growing, having control over your destiny, earning your success, developing quality relationships, and being optimistic about your future—are drivers of happiness. What's really interesting is as we've looked at our paths in becoming authorities and investing in Authority Marketing, we were actually supporting and growing our happiness as well!

In a nutshell, we contend that investing time and resources in Authority Marketing, by making a commitment to becoming a leader and expert in your field, will actually make you a happier person. If you need more convincing, let's start peeling back the layers.

LEARNING AND GROWING

If you were the Authority in your field—the expert when it came to your product or service—you would have to constantly apply yourself and constantly sharpen your sword. The experts of today will not be those of tomorrow unless they continue to learn, grow, and adapt with the changing marketplace and world we live in. You could have been the smartest dentist in the year 2000, but if you haven't constantly learned and grown, by 2020, if not much earlier, you would have been left in the dust. When you make a commitment to be an Authority, it's a commitment to lifelong learning and growing.

CONTROL OVER YOUR DESTINY

Being the go-to Authority gives you more choices, and the more choices you have, the more control over your destiny you have. Wealthy or poor, everyone has problems. In fact, wealthy and poor people share many of the same problems—the difference being that wealthy people have more options and more choices on how to deal with those problems. When you become the expert and Authority, it gives you more options. You're a man or a woman who is now in higher demand, giving you the ability to choose which engagements fulfill you. You're someone whom people now listen to when you speak. You're an individual who now has more influence—someone who is seen as a trusted advisor, not as a salesperson peddling goods. All of which gives you more control over your destiny and that of your company.

EARNED SUCCESS

Becoming an Authority and being seen as a thought leader, unfortunately, doesn't happen overnight. There is no magic pill. There is no potion or formula that will instantly turn you into an Authority. And although that's what so many of us might think we want, we would argue that the journey you undertake in becoming an Authority is more satisfying than the destination. The person you must become to be the go-to leader and expert in your field will give you pride and fulfillment that can last a lifetime. As you embark on this Authority Marketing journey, which will take time, the things you do and the person that you will have to become to be worthy of commanding thought leadership will take significant work. That is the definition of earned success. That is attainment of goals. Perhaps your goal is to be featured in *Forbes* or to be a regular contributor on cable news. Perhaps you want to be invited to keynote the largest industry conference in your field. All these things are goal attainment, and Authority Marketing can help you attain those goals.

QUALITY RELATIONSHIPS

That's all logical, but how in the world does Authority Marketing help you create more quality relationships? At first, it may not seem obvious. However, there are two reasons why this is the case. The first gets back to the media mentality: if you give value first, without any expectation of reciprocation, you become someone who attracts opportunities and good people. Additionally, we would argue that the more Authority you have in your position, the more desirable you are to other people. There's a famous adage that if you put a sign up that says, "Free Puppies" along the side of the road, nobody will stop. But if you put a sign up that says, "Puppies, $500," many will want to stop and take a look. As you become an Authority, as you grow increasingly significant, more people are going to want to participate in your orbit. Our friend Dan Kennedy likes to say, "The higher up in the food chain you go, the more you are paid for who you are rather than what you do." Think about that for a minute: *the more you are paid for who you are rather than what you do.* Well, who can pay more? Oftentimes, the person who can pay more is a strategic relationship or patient. The more you become an Authority, the higher level your sphere of influence and the higher-level circles you begin to run in. That results in higher-level relationships. Believe it or not, we've had authors tell us that becoming Authorities in their fields changed their relationships for the better—including those with their families and loved ones.

OPTIMISTIC FUTURE

Our final driver of happiness, an optimistic future, can also be supported through Authority Marketing. When you become the go-to thought leader, when you have a line of people wrapped around your office wanting to work with you, when you have a clamoring group of people in line to talk to you after you give a speech or a presentation, not only is it fun, but it makes you a magnet for opportunity. The more opportunity you have in your life, the more optimistic you become about the future, and the more you can help others—leading to a more prosperous and fulfilling life.

As we conclude this book, we want to bring the focus onto why everything we have talked about really matters. Yes, it's meant to give you a blueprint to build and market your Authority so you can have a competitive edge in your field, industry, or location. However, success is only a means to an end. The true goal that most people seek to obtain is happiness. When we consider that and look at these major drivers of happiness, it tells us something about the real power of Authority Marketing. We believe taking the journey down this road will be the greatest and most fulfilling decision you can make for your future.

And there has never been a better time than now! The world is changing, and the media landscape is continuing to shift. The power that has traditionally belonged to corporate media giants is now in the hands of every individual for the benefit of anyone who understands how to use it. Now you know how to use it.

In the past only sovereign powers or mainstream media could confer Authority. Today, we live in an era where individuals can confer their own Authority by serving others first. By doing so, dentists, doctors, business owners, entrepreneurs, executives, and thought leaders can gain an outsized advantage on their competition, increase the speed of trust with their customers or patients, and leverage success into greater success.

You now have the knowledge to start leveraging the new media landscape to your advantage. You understand how to develop your

Authority Marketing blueprint and how to implement it. We've broken down the pillars of Authority Marketing for you and we told you that the best way for most people to build Authority is to write a book.

Since success looks different to everyone, that's why Authority Marketing works so well—it's customizable, adaptable, and authentic to who you are and what you do. Whatever means success for you, we hope the Authority Marketing blueprint we have provided here can help support you on the way.

To your success,

Adam & Rusty

AFTERWORD:
THE POWER OF AUTHORITY

by Dan Kennedy, *Founder of Magnetic Marketing*

There is a huge secret about income that only a small percentage of top earners in every field ever figure out and use to their advantage. Most others are ignorant of it, but some see it and, instead of using it, deeply and bitterly resent it. The secret is that the higher up in income you go, in almost any category, the more you are paid for who you are rather than for what you do. That often isn't just, in the way that most people think about justice, and I can't attempt to affect how you think about this in the few words I have for the conclusion to this book, so for now I'll simply state it as the bald fact that it is.

The number-one key to making yourself a powerful, magnetic, trusted, high-income individual, to any target audience or market, is your known and accepted status as an Authority.

BE SEEN AS THE AUTHORITY,
NOT THE SALESPERSON

If you are wandering about in the forest, you will probably recognize a bear if you encounter one. You know bears are big, furry, black or brown, with snouts, and so on. You've seen photos. You've seen them on TV and in movies.

Similarly, you know how to spot a dreaded salesperson in the woods. He has lots of brochures, maybe a PowerPoint presentation on a laptop, sales matter. He usually assaults you and tries to get you to an appointment by various stratagems. In his cubicle or office, there are plaques and trophies proclaiming his sales prowess. Like bears, these sales creatures are to be feared and avoided.

Although I have been a salesman virtually every day of my life, I have gone to great pains not to be perceived as one. Beginning very early in my career to the present, I have implemented an overall marketing strategy to elevate my Authority in the minds of my clientele so that I am not perceived as a salesman. Rather, my business comes to me because *money follows and flows to Authority.*

For me, the journey toward this Authority status began when I first published *The Ultimate Sales Letter* in 1981—a book that has been on bookstore shelves without interruption ever since. It established me as an expert in the craftsmanship of letters that sell. It directly brought me clients, but much more importantly, it elevated my status above other copywriters. People wanted to hear from and get assistance from "the guy who wrote the book" about sales letters, and it is not accidental that the preemptive word "the" is in that title.

I have since written more than thirty books with seven different publishing companies and have gone to considerable effort to effectively implement an ongoing marketing strategy around them, keeping them in print and distribution and using the Authority conveyed by being the author of each book and of an entire series of books to every possible advantage.

Back when I flew commercial—I now travel by private jet—and when I was still on the hunt for clients and business, I always had copies of my books in my carry-on. In 1985, I was in first-class, on a flight from Phoenix to Houston, and the fellow next to me struck up the usual conversation. He identified himself as owner of a Houston-based advertising agency and asked what I did. Instead of an answer or "elevator speech," I stood up, got a copy of *The Ultimate Sales Letter* book, handed it to him, and excused myself for a trip to the bathroom. Two weeks later, I was conducting a nicely compensated training session for his staff copywriters, where he proudly told them, "Today, I have brought you the man who wrote the book on sales-letter writing."

One more story about that first book: the owner of a very large, fast-growing weight-loss company with a hot celebrity endorser, a robust direct-marketing campaign, and distribution in Walmart, brought me to his company headquarters to spend a day discussing direct marketing with his entire staff, followed by a second day working with his three copywriters.

At the start of the first day, he told me he had given *The Ultimate Sales Letter* to everybody a week before so that they would be prepared. He then asked if everybody had read it and announced he was going to conduct a quick, impromptu quiz on the book before I got started. One guy sheepishly admitted he'd been too busy to read the book. My client instantly fired him.

He said, "I've invested in bringing the number-one expert in this field in. If you couldn't invest an hour or two preparing, I do not wish to continue investing in you."

Clients acquire status by having a leading expert working for them. Typically, when prospective clients come to me as a referral, they report that the referring client either told them about one of my books and urged them to get it and read it or gifted them one of my books.

This is what I call the "expert-status halo." People are proud of their association with an expert, be that the number-one expert on home decorating in Abilene or the number-one expert on direct-response marketing and copywriting in the world (me).

MUST YOU SELL OR CAN YOU PRESCRIBE?

Certain experts, professionals, and providers do not sell their recommendations; they have the Authority needed to prescribe.

Authority comes from a matrix of factors, including expert status as well as environment, mindset of customer, criticality of solution, and others. If you have a stomachache that won't go away and hustle over to the local "doc-in-a-box" urgent-care clinic, you'd probably fill a prescription that he issued without question, but you probably wouldn't let him cut you open and remove an organ without a lot of questions; you would demand a second opinion.

However, if your chronic stomach pain takes you from your MD to a specialist at the Cleveland Clinic, who brings in another specialist, and they prescribe urgent surgery, you most likely will sign the form, lie down on the steel cart, and be wheeled away without checking out information via Google.

The solution proposed is the same in both scenarios. *The difference in your reaction is entirely based on your acceptance of the Authority of the person making the recommendation.*

In my own consulting and copywriting practice, I often present complex projects that involve fees from $75,000 to $200,000, plus royalties, and are often more complex and require more investment than a new client has prepared himself for. I never want to have to sell such a thing. I have developed a thorough, carefully choreographed process to avoid having to sell my service.

The following is a brief overview: a potential client typically comes forward from my books, from a referral, from participating in a seminar, or from within Magnetic Marketing membership. The potential client is prevented from contacting me via phone or otherwise and instead is required to fax me a memo describing his business and perceived needs. He first receives a written reply, usually accompanied by one or several of my books. He must then take the initiative to book a consulting day, positioned as "diagnostic and prescriptive" (at my base fee of $18,800).

He may be told of or sent a book of mine to read. He has to travel to me for the day. Before day's end, he is asking me to issue a prescription—which I do. And nine out of ten times it is accepted. This is the power of Authority.

Great Magnetic Marketing members in a very different field, Jeff Giagnocavo and Ben McClure, are authors of *What's Keeping You Up at Night?* and owners of Gardner's Mattress. Their mattresses are priced from $4,000 to $35,000, even while encircled by mattress stores selling at or below the national average of $700.

I am impressed by and very proud of these guys. Everybody else sells mattresses. They prescribe.

In the store, the customer is engaged in a diagnostic conversation. For many, a particular mattress is then prescribed and taken from the showroom floor into the private Dream Room®, a room that mimics a luxury hotel suite, where the customer and spouse spend one, two, or even three hours, nap, watch TV, read, and fully, comfortably experience the chosen bed.

To date, the percentage of customers who buy after trying out the bed in the Dream Room® is—drum roll, please—100 percent. This is the power of Authority. One of the Magnetic Marketing members in my top coaching program is Steve Adams, the owner of twenty-one exceptionally profitable retail pet stores. In each store, there is a professional pet-nutrition counselor who engages customers in a diagnostic process to then prescribe the best customized diet and food for that person's pet. The total customer value and retention is much, much higher than ordinary stores manage.

That's the power of Authority.

If you want to be liberated from selling, if you want to prescribe rather than sell, then you need to focus on building your status, building your Authority, and becoming the leader in your field.

THE IRRATIONAL REACTION TO STAR POWER

Recently, there have been two supremely successful TV ad campaigns that you probably saw ad nauseam: one for an herbal prostate remedy, starring former NFL quarterback Joe Theismann, the other for investing in gold, starring the gray-haired, rugged-looking actor William Devane.

These campaigns minted money with star power, because people react irrationally to celebrities and celebrity endorsements. And at all levels, NetJets' sales improved as soon as Warren Buffett bought the company. Warren is a rich-person's celebrity. He is not an expert in air travel safety. Levitra® was made popular beginning with ads starring former Chicago Bears coach Mike Ditka, a cigar-chomping tough guy, a man's man, but not an expert on medicine.

If people were rational, it would be better to promote NetJets with a highly credentialed expert in aircraft maintenance and to promote Levitra® with a top doctor from the Harvard Medical School.

I have used star power by association, rented star power, and manufactured star power throughout my business life, with celebrity endorsements from the likes of Joan Rivers and Fox Business economics expert Harry Dent. Top celebrity speakers such as Brian Tracy and Tom Hopkins have written introductions to books for me, and I even got an endorsement from a contestant on President Donald Trump's former TV show *The Apprentice*, in which she says, "Even Donald Trump could learn a thing or two from Dan's book."

My Authority status is what draws 1,000 to 1,500 entrepreneurs to our major Magnetic Marketing events, and I welcome those that buy six, eight, twenty books to be autographed and given to friends because they're working as a subtle sales force, reaching lots of people I might never reach otherwise, at no out-of-pocket cost, bringing new customers to Magnetic Marketing and occasionally a client to me.

This Authority status also draws others to me, who want to be associated with me through endorsements or even coauthorship of a book, because this allows them to position themselves further in their own fields as experts and authorities.

I have also gotten a lot of speaking engagements on programs where I've appeared—often repeatedly—with an eclectic collection of political, business, and world leaders, and Hollywood and sports celebrities. I've spent nine years with the famous SUCCESS events (held in sports arenas with audiences of 10,000 to 35,000), and I've attended many clients' events.

I often urge clients to hire celebrity speakers; at Magnetic Marketing events, where we always use at least one celebrity-entrepreneur, the list has included Gene Simmons (KISS), Joan Rivers, Ivanka Trump, John Rich (winner, *Celebrity Apprentice*), and Barbara Corcoran (*Shark Tank*).

Because of my plan, I have been able to work with a lot of impressive people whose names should arguably not influence others' thinking about my value as an advisor on business or marketing matters. There is no rational link between my appearing on programs with these people and my expertise and trustworthiness as someone to tell you how to invest your money in advertising and marketing.

It should not be influential. But it is.

AUTHORITY MARKETING: THE TRIFECTA OF MAGNETIC ATTRACTION AND RISING INCOME

If you wish to achieve fame and status in your field, you must design and implement an Authority Marketing plan that includes multiple strategies—often including book authorship—to position yourself as an undisputed expert, influential Authority, and in-demand celebrity.

When you combine standout expertise (which many have), with the visibility of celebrity (which some have), you become an Authority (which few are). These two factors, working in concert, act to deliver three very desirable benefits: you are made able to more readily attract more and better clients/customers, make selling to them easier, and make price less of an issue so that the profitability of your business improves.

How do you become an Authority most effectively and efficiently? With the power of Authority Marketing.

Dan Kennedy, *Founder*
Magnetic Marketing|No B.S. Inner Circle (MagneticMarketing.com)

**PARTIAL LIST OF CELEBRITIES, AUTHORS, BUSINESS LEADERS & OTHERS
DAN KENNEDY HAS APPEARED ON PROGRAMS WITH AS A SPEAKER**

Political & World Leaders
President Gerald Ford
President Ronald Reagan
President George Bush
President Donald Trump
Gen. Norman Schwarzkopf
Secretary Colin Powell
Mikail Gorbachev
Lady Margaret Thatcher
William Bennett
Legendary Entrepreneurs
Mark McCormack
Sports Agent, Founder IMG, Author,
What They Don't Teach You At
Harvard Business School)
Ben & Jerry *(Ben & Jerry's Ice Cream)*
Debbi Fields *(Mrs. Fields Cookies)*
Jim McCann *(1-800-Flowers)*
Joe Sugarman *(Blu-Blockers)*
**Hollywood Personalities &
Entertainers**
Johnny Cash
Naomi Judd
Mary Tyler Moore
Christopher Reeve
The Smothers Brothers
Willard Scott
Barbara Walters
Charlton Heston
Broadcasters
Larry King
Paul Harvey
Deborah Norville

Authors & Speakers
Zig Ziglar *(See You At The Top)*
Brian Tracy
Jim Rohn
Tom Hopkins
Mark Victor Hansen
(Chicken Soup For The Soul)
Tony Robbins *(Unlimited Power)*
Mike Vance *(Dean, Disney Univ.;*
Think Outside The Box)
Michael Gerber *(E-Myth)*
**Sports Personalities,
Athletes & Coaches**
Joe Montana
Troy Aikman
Peyton Manning
Mike Singletary
Coach Tom Landry
Coach Jimmy Johnson
Coach Lou Holtz
Dick Vitale
George Foreman
Muhammad Ali
Mary Lou Retton
Bonnie Blair
Dan Jansen
Other Newsmakers
Lt. Col. Oliver North
Gerry Spence
Alan Dershowitz
Capt. Scott O'Grady
Health
Dr. Ted Broer
Dr. Jack Groppel

ABOUT THE AUTHORS

ADAM WITTY
Founder and Chief Executive Officer

Adam Witty is the founder and CEO of Advantage Media Group, Business Journals Books, and ForbesBooks, The Business Growth Company. Advantage|Business Journals Books|ForbesBooks, which began in the spare bedroom of Witty's home, boasts a roster of 1,500 Members all 50 US states and 63 countries. Started in 2005, Advantage and its other publishing imprints have helped busy professionals become the Authority in their field through publishing and marketing. Adam is publisher of *Authority Magazine* and *ForbesBooks Review* and the host of the Authority Summit, the largest annual conference on authority marketing. Advantage has been named to the Inc. 500|5000 list of the fastest growing companies in America in 2012, 2013, 2014, 2016, 2017, and 2018 and *The Best Places to Work in South Carolina* list for 2013, 2014, and 2015.

In 2016, Advantage launched a historic partnership with Forbes, one of the most iconic business media companies in the world, to create ForbesBooks, a business book publisher for top business leaders. In 2019, Advantage partnered with the largest local business media company in the world, American City Business Journals, to launch the new imprint Business Journals Books, buoyed by the strength of 43 weekly business journals in the top markets in America.

Adam is the author of seven books including *Looking Forward to Monday, Lead The Field, 21 Ways to Build Your Business With a Book,* and *Book The Business: How to Make Big Money With Your Book Without Even Selling a Single Copy,* the top book on marketing for authors that he coauthored with marketing legend Dan Kennedy.

Adam is a sought-after speaker, teacher, and consultant on marketing and business growth techniques for entrepreneurs and authors. Adam has shared the stage with Alan Mulally, Steve Forbes, Gene Simmons of KISS, Peter Guber, and Bobby Bowden. Adam has been featured in *The Wall Street Journal, Investors Business Daily, USA Today,* and on ABC and Fox. Adam has been named to Charleston's Forty Under 40, 50 Most Progressive, and was named to the 2011 *Inc.* Magazine 30 Under 30 list of "America's coolest entrepreneurs." In 2012, Adam was selected by the Chilean government to judge the prestigious Start-up Chile! entrepreneurship competition.

Adam is chairman of not-for-profit Youth Entrepreneurship South Carolina that teaches entrepreneurial skills to at-risk youth in every South Carolina public school. Adam is chairman of Clemson University's Spiro Entrepreneurship Institute and serves on the board of the College of Charleston Entrepreneurship Center. Adam is a pilot, Eagle Scout, 2012 Clemson University Young Alumnus of the Year, and a member of Young Presidents' Organization (YPO), Entrepreneurs' Organization (EO), and Tiger 21. He is happy to call Charleston, South Carolina home.

You can connect with Adam directly at AdamWitty.com.

RUSTY SHELTON
Senior Marketing Strategist

Rusty Shelton first spoke at Harvard on the changing world of PR and marketing at the age of twenty-three.

He is a senior marketing strategist and publisher at Advantage|Business Journals Books|ForbesBooks. He is also the founder and CEO of Zilker Media and cofounder of Catch Engine, the country's leading quiz marketing software platform.

He is the coauthor, alongside Barbara Cave Henricks, of *Mastering the New Media Landscape: Embrace the Micromedia Mindset*, which is endorsed by David Meerman Scott, Tom Rath, Sally Hogshead, and many others.

Rusty's commentary on the changing world of PR and marketing has been featured in *Forbes, Inc. Magazine*, *Wharton*, *The Huffington Post*, and many other top media outlets.

A successful entrepreneur, Rusty built and sold two businesses before the age of thirty-five, including Shelton Interactive, which he founded in 2010 and worked with his team to grow into one of the nation's most respected digital marketing agencies prior to its acquisition by Advantage|Business Journals Books|ForbesBooks in 2016. Shelton Interactive handled the launch of more than thirty *New York Times* and *Wall Street Journal* bestsellers and represented some of the world's most recognized authorities. The company was also named one of the nation's top ten social media marketing agencies in 2014 and 2015 by research agency Clutch.

An active keynote speaker, Rusty speaks regularly at top conferences and leads workshops for businesses of every size. He has spoken at EO Alchemy, SXSW Interactive, and the Financial Planning Conference.

You can connect with Rusty directly at www.RustyShelton.com.

Visit us online to access these free resources:

Find Out Your Patient Relationship Score.

We've created a simple 9 Question Assessment that will reveal your Patient Relationship Score in under 3 minutes, and share with you exactly how you can quickly improve your score.

→ Take the Patient Relationship Assessment by visiting at mlivesoftware.com/assessment.

SUBSCRIBE to Dental Marketing Live.

You've learned about the Seven Pillars of Authority Marketing, now stay on top of the latest marketing trends and strategies with the mLive Dental Marketing weekly newsletter. Read articles and latest dental industry trends to stay on top of your marketing efforts.

→ Subscribe at mlivesoftware.com/newsletter.

Book a Complimentary Demo of our mLive Software.

Learn how you can easily attract and win over more, new, and better patients with our bold, persuasive automated marketing campaigns. mLive Dental Marketing Automation software does all this and more so you can put your marketing on autopilot.

→ Schedule today at mlivesoftware.com/demo.

Printed in the USA
CPSIA information can be obtained
at www.ICGtesting.com
JSHW012033140824
68134JS00033B/3040